Maple Window

Craig Reger

Copyright 2011 by Craig Reger

Palindrome Publishers

Editors: Judith Skretny, William Reger

Table of Contents

Preface

Looking out this window day after day with my mother at my side makes me feel lucky that I have a mother so warm and caring; I wish I could whisper to her as much.

Not every child is supposed to be born. The naturally selective process determines that the strongest survive. I was supposed to be born because I am here. Birthing is the first earthly right of passage in a selective process that has been in place for (b) millions of years. I will pass on to infinity when I am no longer strong enough like every other living breathing animal. Since I am here I feel obliged to tell you why I am here and what "here" is from the perspective of my societal sub-culture. May's Window is my attempt to pass on an assimilated form of myself, in a book if you will, because self-perpetuation is not possible for me.

My parents were not aware of my genetic deficiencies in utero. Mom was asked once would she have terminated her pregnancy if she knew. Some would call that murder and some would call it sympathy. I refer to it as the most humane decision a parent can make.

I am not "writing" this book out of self pity I am "writing" for the sake of "writing". It is cathartic, energizing, and necessary for me. Pity should be saved for the mirthless and others who do not take advantage of the fact that it is a wonder we are even here.

Being classified as a retard, idiot, dumb, haphazard, or delayed is not hurtful to me. I am quite ambivalent towards the stigma of my being. Those are classifications based on my lack of response to invoked stimuli. It doesn't mean I am not stimulated, it means my response is muted.

Thank you to my father for helping me with the typing. My mother's strength of will is un-fleeting and it makes this book possible. Everybody in my family plays a role in the window to the world for me, Olivia May Reger, otherwise known as "Little May".

Lightning Crashes

Chapter 1

Hi, my name is Olivia May. I was born with a genetic defect which has affected my ability to talk, walk, and communicate verbally throughout my adventures of life. My conceptual shortcomings have allowed me the paradoxical benefit of absorbing a unique perspective on life that I observe from a rather quiet, supine, and undisturbed observational angle.

My anticipation of a shorter life span (something less than 67.2 years) has been a wonderful tool to help me aggregate my daily energy for respectable mental and physical utility. Disregarding medical advances I suspect my chances for leading a productive life are equivalent to the following:

Imagine for a moment you are a child and have been inadvertently left behind in the forest during a family camping trip. You have no use of your arms and legs, and blurred vision grants paralyzing fear to your disconsolate thoughts of accidental abandonment. Your family silently waits for news about your safe return from weary volunteer search crews. Some family members silently pray to God for a miracle. A calloused news team interviews your mother as she pleads for your safe return over the airwaves. The story can end in only one way. An angry thunder storm halts the search crew efforts as lightening crashes and an old giant oak tree succumbs to the heavy wind and stinging rain. You see a giant shadow cross the moonlit sky at the last moment. Your life ends before living could begin. These are the odds I face in my attempt to return to the warm dancing campfire.

An evening sky through my bedroom window reminds me of a dancing campfire as I watch stars self-immolate throughout the night. Green grass is comfortable for me because I know I cannot fall any further when I am lying in the soft warm grass. A blue sky leaves me in a transcendental state of wonderment. After a summer afternoon in my backyard I am left to wonder how I even got here and what my meaning for being here is. Supposing there is tangible meaning to any of us being here on planet earth.

My life has tangible meaning to my family and should add up to something but not in what I have at the end, because it won't be much, but what I gave throughout my life to my family by way of small unspoken gifts. This book, my smile, my easy nature, my willingness to compromise, and my desire to sleep in on weekends to give mom a break are other small gifts.

My greatest desire is self-expression, other than living, I suppose. Life is a wonderful party if invited. I am not a VIP so I wait my turn behind the velvet ropes. I have found it easier to decipher lethargic strangers and their transparent desires than expose my well-hidden aspirations.

At a daily minimum I aspire to an illusory happiness. If that illusion keeps my sanity, then I will hold onto that illusion as conciliatory happiness for what could have been for me. My potential may have been reached in life, and it is not because I have set the bar low for my goals.

Out of the millions of people who could have been me it turned out to be me. If it wasn't me I will always be curious if it would have still been me. There certainly could have been better more worthwhile productive Olivias (just not as pretty) but that is how natural selection works. If a certain other DNA were selected, this book might not be here.

God moves in a mysterious way his wonders to perform (English poet, William Cowper). Possibly God put me here to write this book. Is this a lesser book than what I could have co-written with

Dad had I been born healthy? I will try and find the right time in my life to ask for an apology from a not so humble God on his performance (or lack thereof) in creating me. It is not required of my humble lost soul to accept god's apology. I tolerate my deprecated physical contraction and social stigma with the knowledge that God's intervention to assist would be unimpeded by me.

People with my physical condition are often understood only to the limited capacity that humans can visually infer. Ah! The political incorrectness associated with stereotypes. Muslims in an airport representing religious fundamentalism, trailer parks in Central Florida representing illiterate un-educated country people, and construction companies in New Jersey representing la Cosa Nostra are all common stereotypes that society is quick to judge. I certainly don't have the same physical and mental capacity as "normal" humans, but I do have tangible qualities of fortitude and an unbent morality that others would appreciate more if it could be tested.

I don't have a problem with my social stature. Society has a problem with me. I am not uncomfortable in a crowd. The crowd is uncomfortable with stereotypical me. It is easy to lump me into the lowest social scale and conclude that I will be physically useless the rest of my days. It is easy to say because it is true. I fit the stereotype of a thoughtless physically challenged haphazard the same way as aforementioned stereotypes are vilified as evil, illiterate moonshiners, and/or immoral. The same way Muslims will not stop using airports I will not stop unintentionally impeding traffic at restaurants, museums, and libraries at the behest of the many more mobile members of society.

In fact, I will be a physical impediment and financial burden on my family, state, and country for the foreseeable future. I am here to write about what I can bring to the table of the good earth through my quick written wit and not my fast spoken word. If I had to choose I would much rather have quick wit than a fast tongue. I don't consider these types of hypothetical choices very worthwhile to me, other than amusing. Hypothetically speaking, my teaching voice probably would have been drowned out by other monotone redemption seeking poets, novelists, and songwriters guilty of axioms far worse than being born a certain way.

The maxim "she has taught us so much" is overextended in our family's case and suggests that my mother and father were a rebellious pair who were ultimately saved by my sovereign grace. I am not discounting my arrival and medical discovery as a seminal moment in their lives but my compromised genotype did highlight their tough resilient predispositions to the outside world. Their parenting does not go by the book "How to cope with a special needs child". Justly, I would like some credit in helping to introduce a tidal wave of new information and terminology for them to process. My failure to thrive helped them gather medical wisdom like old western sagebrush rolls up dust. Sacrifice seems like a cruel means of enlightenment even according to my interrupted brain but as long as my parents learn from it and share their discoveries I am fine with this sacrifice.

Continuing on about myself, my brain function is vulnerable to disorganization. Moving my arms, legs, and head without seemingly obvious purpose can be tiresome, and burn much needed calories. I don't want to move my limbs, but sometimes I just can't stop. I move my head rhythmically from side to side to get a sense of what and who is around me. I cry a smidgen more than the new breed of technologically spoiled over protected child. I never cry of self pity. Crying usually emanates from intestinal discomfort or respiratory illness but not always in that order. Have you ever been constipated for eight days? Not having consistent peristalsis is a real bummer (sorry, had to say it). I do have an acquired sense of humor like my father's. I try to be more discerning about applying my humor in social settings than my father is.

If you ever thought you had a rough day, you should re-think your definition of "rough day". Thinking my own thoughts is what gets me through the day when I am lucky enough to be resting in the most comfortable spot in the world, on my Dad's shoulder. The beauty of my lack of physical abilities is that I have the time and space to retrieve my thoughts and personal interpretations about what is happening around me without having combed the landscape of physical experience. I have looked through the eyes of mom and learned from her humility. I have looked through the eyes of Dad and felt his victories and felt his anguish from his losses. I can only hope my descriptions of personal interactions with strangers, friends, and family members, gives you a chance to learn from someone who is unlearned.

For example, on the subject of family workings I am perplexed how a mother and father can have the opposite impact on their children during similar existential experiences. I embrace my Dad at the dinner table while I sense anxiousness from Jeremy and Cassandra my big brother and big sister. The conclusion being that I abide by Mom and Dad for the simple treasure of being fed for my continued existence. I enjoy eating and it keeps me alive. Jeremy and Cassandra eat dinner, including the required vegetables so they are not a statistic at the hands of Dad. I eat to live they eat not to die.

My older brother and older sister understand what it means to not sweat the small stuff (sometimes). I will take credit for this aspect of their life (sometimes) because of my often times close vicarious relationship with the rapid onset of illness.

Jeremy is the oldest, and is never slow to present his intangibles. Jeremy is a leader, effusively bright, handsome (like his dad), and not one to ignore the impact of his actions. Jeremy is the consummate big brother and son.

My older sister Cassandra has a brilliant mind that is a silhouette of her life's enormous potential. She has generously offered me a ride as her personal passenger during her intellectual journey through life.

Dad was always a bit different. He is not a man of conventional thought process. Dad doesn't see the bright side of a loss or the virtues of a moral victory. Dad doesn't need a moral victory. He has accomplished that already. It was always a win or a loss for Dad when he played sports. It's not "how you play the game" or playing to "have fun" for Dad because it wasn't fun losing. (I hope he notices the past tense). Give it up Dad, you can't outrun old age. Cassandra will argue with Dad that sports should be about fun. If you are not having fun why play? "When I win I have fun". And so it goes, until Cassandra wins the argument. Relinquishing to an opposing side during an "animated discussion" is not something anybody in this family does with charity.

Dad has bestowed the value of athletic competition on his children. Reaching into the unknowns of your physical abilities during competition can leave a lasting impression on your future endeavors and help build the bank of resiliency deposits to be removed in the future on an as needed basis. I am the exception to that athletic endowment. Dad would freely admit that he harbors pain in the fact he will never see me run. Living can be more memorable when you can run full speed with all your vigor, strength, and determination.

Dad did not want to know our gender and did not want to pick out the names before our births. He had to see a face and body. Dad *had* to understand visually what he was going to deal with for the next 50-60 years of his life. Dad wasn't looking for the latest name craze or naming his children based on his expectations for his children. Dad felt like he should name his children based on his first visuals. (That is usually the course of action with an expected litter of pups or kittens).

Mom was always trying to have name choice discussions with Dad. It was an exciting time for mom to think about possible names and to discuss favorite names with Dad and all her friends. Every article in the paper or current best-selling book had a name mom was interested in. She looked at name tags of employees in department stores, solicitors as they phoned the house were queried on their names, and of course carrying down certain family names had genial relevance. Dad's naming discussion technique was based on a plan to delay, ignore, and stay feebly occupied during the discussion so as to leave mom no choice but to wait for the birth and hope her mentally prepared chart of names would be one of the chosen names. Suffice it to say her names weren't on the final list of names after birth. Surprisingly, mom couldn't fit some of her favorite names with the new face. After a couple of days the nurses would say, "Mr. and Mrs. Reger, we need a name for the birth certificate". I think the three Reger children had question marks on the cribs in the neonatal units until the state demanded to know a name for its paperwork. Having a question mark on the name plate in my crib certainly is an ironic way to capture the beginning days of my life.

I suppose Dad looked at me as Olympian when he first suggested the name "Olympia" to mom as he scoured my appearance for name clues. Dad would ultimately disclose that he noticed a new housing development sign across the street from the hospital room view. The new development name was "Olympia". Mom wasn't very excited about naming her daughter after a real estate development. Dad felt like it was a clever name that suited my speedy arrival and potential javelin throwing prowess.

Mom coerced the name Olivia as a reasonable compromise. She really liked the name Olivia when she first said it, and Dad turned his head when he heard it for the first time. Introducing, Olivia May. I enjoy the regal sound and feel to my name. I always wondered if my name was on a highly secured list of names my mother never discussed with dad. Mom knew the relative hopelessness of naming discussions with Dad. I tend to think Olivia was in her bullpen of unannounced names. She is too smart not to be duly unprepared with naming rights at her third child's birth.

Suffice it to say, the naming rights to the three of us were bartered off rather uneventfully. Outdoor signage, anniversaries of movie classics, and just plain old conversational attrition bequeathed us our names.

On average, men are more visual than women. Mom is a bit more pragmatic. She wanted the bedrooms painted the appropriate gender colors (with borders), names picked out, furniture purchased, gender colored clothes purchased, and college lists prepared.

I love the story of when Dad and Mom were trying to have their first child. It was taking longer than they hoped so Dad lugged Mom out of bed at 5am on a Sunday and proceeded to the beach (they lived in South Florida) for a Sunday Morning of Champagne, Orange juice and a beautiful sunrise. Mom says it may be the most (only) romantic thing Dad has ever done! After the sunrise and several orange juice cocktails, seven months later Jeremy was born.

Jeremy is Mom and Dad's medical prequel to me. Jeremy was delivered two months early at the distressing weight of three pounds and a few Lincolns. Jeremy had complications with breathing because his lungs had not been developed enough to handle the re-circulated hospital air. Sixteen days in the neo-natal intensive care unit (NICU) and some tense moments sure set the table for Mom's strategy for dealing with doctors, nurses, insurance companies and the ennui of dealing with hospital administrators.

Heartbreakingly for Dad, he missed Jeremy's birth. Mom had sent him home from the hospital in the morning to get some of her belongings. Mom was taken in the night before because her water had burst, but she was given morphine to try to keep Jeremy in because of his small size and potential inadequate lung capacity. The steroids seemed to have worked. Mom really had to have HER toothbrush though. Dad thought it was strange timing to the request but in the same light it was not a good time to argue. Dad received a call while at the house after picking up the toothbrush and sped back to the hospital in morning rush hour on the wrong side of the road many times. He had missed the birth by one minute, but Mom had clean teeth after the birth.

Dad learned from his mistake. In the near future dad would not miss Cassandra's birth or mine. Conspicuously missing from my birth was a reason.

A Broken Window
Chapter 2

My apgar levels at birth were low. Apgar scores are based on skin color, pulse rate, muscle tone, reflex and breathing. Coincidently, I may have broken a record for shortest labor time. The nurses had to suction fluid from my throat as I was not breathing for a short spell from the umbilical cord acting as a tourniquet around my neck. It is hard to say how long I was having difficulty breathing. Mom's total labor time with me was under 45 minutes. That sequence of events is my parent's best reference point as to possibly why I am like I am today. Not breathing reduces blood flow and oxygen to the brain which in turn can induce a brain injury.

A few hours later, the nurses sanitized me and handed me to my mom. That whole birthing, anti-septic process seems like an apartment moving episode where the cleaners come in to get ready for the next renter. I liked the apartment complex I was in. I wasn't ready to upsize. Soon after, mom was to hang her vacancy sign. Metaphorically speaking that is. She didn't know it at the time, but I was going to be her third and last born child.

I am sure I felt I should be in mom's arms in the hospital. That is how I feel today when mom cuddles me. Our hearts beat rhythmically. Its' astonishing the oneness I feel with Mom. I realize I was too young to remember the emotional hospital setting but it is nice to reflect back and feel those emotions today that surely we felt simultaneously long ago.

Moms are what drive children out to face the improvements each day the earth brings. It is not an intricate relationship. It is an elastic relationship that evolves through time based on product, service, supply, and demand. It is the most economical relationship imaginable. It is a relationship that is self-regulating, self- sustaining, and has no replacement parts available at the hardware store. I have always felt it is more important that my mother is who she is rather than what she does. Who she is drives what she does. Dads, well can we just call them uncomfortable creatures until their children are able to speak (myself un-included). Dads get put on hold while Moms jump into the natural role they require no training for.

My apgar tests improved during the next testing. Mom says they improved because she got a hold of me and I slept with her in her hospital bed. "Home Schooling" usually results in brighter test scores for children. Draw your own conclusions. Testing has always been difficult for me because testing requires a response output. Testing requires me to search my strands of memory and my experiences and then somehow attach my usually correct answer to a form of communication which I do not possess.

Two weeks into my life, Mom became troubled because I didn't like to open my engaging blue eyes almost from birth and I became a real challenge in the breast feeding arena. My vexed mother would be up all night trying to get me to feed. Mom was always insistent on breast feeding her children. The immunological and cognitive advantages are well known in the medical community and by experienced mothers across the globe. Breast feeding helped facilitate calmness in my daily life. I liked having a satisfied belly as all babies do, and breast feeding reinforced the strong bond that mom and I shared.

Latching on with consistency was the biggest obstacle for me. I would forget how to breastfeed from day to day. Mom never was sure what she was going to get out of me when we sat down to feed. Mom says I had the baby instincts to attempt feeding but most attempts would end prematurely in frustration on both parts due to my inability to latch on. This went on for a month or so, I was feeding enough, but it was an arduous task for Mom and me.

After a month of practicing all hours of the day and night I figured out breastfeeding. I had to figure it out. Mom was exhausted from the frequent manual pumping to relieve her pain. It was a very frustrating time for mom because she knew breast feeding was so important and it was such a soothing experience for me when I could temporarily latch on. It was a matter of consistency for me. I suppose in some way I could feel Mom's frustration and her anxiety.

It just happened one day. I spent a whole day breastfeeding with no setbacks. It was like an alarm went off in my brain to alert me that it was time to understand the importance of my task. Mom got some sleep that night, and I loved my new job so much I didn't ever want to clock out. I continued to breast feed for the next 6-7 months. When you work at something everyday for many hours a day in a repetitious manner ultimately successes will be realized.

Riding in our automobile was another object of my desire. If Dad was too tired to drive he would throw me over his shoulder and walk around for hours while mom got some medically necessary relief from me. Dad would sleep walk, which was a bit safer than sleep driving. An automobile, as many parents of sleep resistant babies will attest to, will reduce a child to slumber with the humming sounds and light bouncing action that neutralizes even the most colicky baby.

Friends and family would say I was a colicky baby. Meaning I would cry for some unexplained reason. As you will learn about my father he would say if my current malady can be asserted without explanation to him, he can ignore a flimsy diagnosis without his own counter explanation. The word colic was not in his vocabulary because it was considered "unexplained crying". How could crying be unexplainable? Mom would tell the pediatrician my stomach hurts. The pediatrician would emphatically respond that I was just colicky. Mom would say OK, how can we figure out the ongoing stomach pain? The Dr. would respond that I would eventually calm down and that I was just being colicky. Mom would then say it has been six months and the doctor referral merry-go-round would ensue. Incidentally, Adults don't cry inexplicably except if you're a fan of the Buffalo Bills. Point being that there must be a reason for my crying.

At my two month pediatric visit the Doctor told Mom that I looked dysmorphic. Dysmorphic is a medical term that can suggest a possible genetic abnormality. Mom was concerned not insulted by the dysmorphic statement. The pediatrician suggested that my ears were a bit lower than usual and that my eyes had a "sunset" look to them. My heavy eyes were usually closed. Mom didn't think I was hitting my milestones and couldn't reconcile the fact that I cried most of the time. Mom always had larger goals than the average milestone accumulation for her children, so she pursued the conversation because she felt I should have been more active on my belly. The end result of that pulverizing conversation to my family's future was to get a genetic test done on me. Mom always appreciates the medical professionals being candid with their conversation. There still is value in telling the truth these days.

Apparently, when your ears are a little lower than your eyes you are dysmorphic, who knew! Having ears that work seems more important than placement. I might be a new line of naturally selected lowered ear human beings. Ears lower to the ground I suppose would allow for oncoming aggressors to be heard from greater distances. Look at me, rationalizing a supposed birth defect into greater appreciation for gene modification.

My family's ancestry doesn't support any history of genetic abnormality concerns. As far as we can tell there are not any genetic aberrations on either side of the family.

Dad would come home from work after a long day at one of his restaurants and try to play with me by throwing me over his head. I am not saying this to get children's services coming for a visit. There must be a statute of limitations in play here. I didn't like it at all, and would cry. Dad felt something different with me than with Jeremy and Cassie when they were young. Dad confided in me that something might be wrong with me, but he didn't address it outside of asking me, and I was just a twelve week old baby. There were a few other signs. At night, I just couldn't stop moving. Mom would study me and wonder when I was going to fall asleep. Mom was a veteran, me being her third child she knew I shouldn't be moving rhythmically for hours at a time. The signs were there, both parents seemed to recognize a unique-ness in me through their own private interactions with me. Mom wasn't going to throw me in the air and Dad wasn't going to be up with me at 3am after working eighteen hours. And thus, the conscious decoding of Little May had begun. Dad nick-named me Little May which is better than dismay because I was so tiny. I only gained 2 pounds in the first two months of my tumultuous life.

My first "episode" came as a shock to my mother. Mom wasn't so sure it was a seizure at that moment, but in hind-sight it was determined to be a seizure. We were visiting West Seneca, New York (outside of Buffalo) for my baptism at Queen of Heaven Church and School in Dad's hometown. My brother and sister were baptized in this same Church. My Dad grudgingly went to grammar school at Queen of Heaven, some two hundred years ago or thereabouts! We were not a religious family but at the time it seemed like a harmless request to fulfill to have a chance to enter the Catholic version of eternity. The majority of Mom and Dad's family religious provenance is Catholic and most of the grandparents were excited about the prospect of baptism for me and all of their grandchildren. Obviously, we all want to be able to spend eternity together (right?). Baptisms are a great excuse for a party, and my family certainly doesn't shy away from a gathering that may or may not contain fermented beverages and a gaggle of musical instruments.

How exciting, so many story lines in one day. It seems strange to have water dumped on my head and be forgiven for my sins. What could I have done to sin at my age? I am sold that sins are handed down through the ages like Cassie's christening outfit given to me. Doesn't seem fair, but so it goes.

After the ceremony we drove out to the country to Mimi and Grandpas summer home. It was such a warm balmy day, the sun felt so nice on my face. Dad had the rental car sun roof open. Whenever something is wrong I always feel better with a little sun on my face and wind in my hair. Don't you? The sun on this day felt extra soothing after the salty sting of holy water in my eyes.

At the summer country home, Mom and I were having alone time and talking about shopping and getting our hair and nails done. Mom's happy place is shopping at large department stores that rhyme with jarget. Suddenly, during feeding time without warning my whole body began to stiffen as my knees pulled up to my chest, my eyes rolled to the side, and my lips turned blue. Mom held me and observed the thirty second interruption without summoning for help. Her sense of calm during a storm is a quality that has built her an unassailable reputation throughout her professional career. Mom was fearful that I was choking, but the sudden exit from my distress ended before applicable choking measures could be taken. Choking while breast feeding? Mom was cautiously weighing what she had witnessed and circumstances surrounding.

Mom wasn't sure how to explain that episode to Dad. Mom was scared, worried, but very calm. She told Dad something had occurred that resembled what Mom felt like was choking but the theory didn't support the observation. Dad pondered, never one to state the obvious obligatory next question in a conversation of "Are you sure"? "Where did you lose your keys"?

Uneasiness colored mom's thoughts. She had a difficult time explaining what she saw and she was lacking witnesses to the affair, other than me. A distant part of mom's brain thought of the pediatrician's dysmorphic statement, the constant colicky, and the missing milestones. What did it all mean was a succinct question to ponder.

Mom gave me to Aunt Tammy a short while later and relieved herself to the bathroom. When we visit Mimi and Grandpa's house in the country and use the bathroom we do it with reserved anxiousness because of what might be hanging on the inside bathroom door. Mom threw some cold fresh spring water on her face and felt like crying when alone and seeing my eyes looking back through the mirror. Could Olivia have been choking Mom asked her-self?

Seizures hijack my mind for a spell sometimes. I feel as though I am falling through the sky not able to breathe because of the onrushing wind and other times enveloped in warm water with air un-accessible as sounds are muffled all around. The jarring convulsions are a slow motion attack on my sense of surrounding. I am whisked away by land, other times by sea with arms outstretched for mom but she can't reach me.

I listen to my parents talk about my seizures afterwards if I am still awake. There is a mental moment of bliss just before a seizure. The calm before the storm I suppose. Where it comes from or what it means, I am not sure. Seizures certainly don't look like bliss, but it seems to me they are a bit more disconcerting for the people who are the witnesses rather than for the patient. Funny thing is I usually feel better after a seizure. I feel like my body and brain have rid themselves of a foreign invader that was disrupting my eco-system.

There was no questioning the brilliant summer day. The wine was aged and the breeze was soothing to the brow. Mom didn't put me down the rest of the day, even if somebody asked to hold the newly christened beauty. Seizures and/or unexplained choking were not something mom had ever witnessed or was even faintly familiar with. Mom played the caution card with me from this day forward.

Mom doesn't like the unknown: when it comes to her children she is on top of her game with her children. Not quite the disciplinarian, but she can unequivocally throw the love around, softie that she is. Mom leaves the brute force up to Dad. Dad has a *bark worse than his bite*. All of the sudden he hits his limit with no warning and BAM – No X-box, and everybody is getting shipped to Africa, India or the west side of Buffalo to learn a lesson on how lucky we are to have running water. He gives everybody space to sort out the disagreements. As Dad likes to say to Jeremy and Cassandra, "I am not your problem solver". Mom and Dad create a balance based on these different approaches to parenting in our house. It may not be too different in your home. Every home has its own unique way of raising children. Your house is uniquely your home when this inevitable interaction occurs. Since a home in America has 2.2 children, this uniqueness probably occurs eight hundred and three times a year (not including leap year)

After returning to the sweltering heat of Florida and the always unpredictable hurricane season mom and I visited the pediatrician. I had another "choking" session shortly after returning home. The pediatrician said I was more than likely choking. Mom wasn't convinced of his unconvincing tone nor could she understand how I could choke on liquids. The next doctor reiterated the pediatrician's analysis as choking. Mom decided to videotape the next choking episode.

It was confirmed to be a seizure after mom showed the doctor a videotape. The seizures began to increase in volume and intensity a few weeks after we returned to Florida especially during hurricanes.

How do meteorologists decide on the number of hurricanes to strike each year? Is nature that predictable? Is it through the previous year's activities? I digress. High pressure hurricanes are like a vice grip on my brain. Unfortunately, medical help is not available for home emergencies through 9-1-1 during hurricanes as mom and dad frighteningly found out during my first encounter with the swirling hedonists of hubris! Mom and Dad had to rely on each other to get me through my cranium vapor locks in a candle lit room. The ensuing power loss, inevitable water contamination, and insufferable heat proved equally challenging. Moms find a way, don't they? My mom found the air-conditioned mall to keep us all cool while dad went about cleanup and repairs.

These days seizures make me sleepy afterwards, which is just as well because if I am sleeping I usually won't seize up again, unless I am in what is called a cluster of seizures. The seizures began to be a routine part of my life after three months of age. I would have fifteen to thirty seizures a day. Mom and Dad began to videotape them for doctors to review. I wouldn't always have seizures on cue at the Doctors office so it became necessary to create a log of when, where, and how long each seizure lasted.

There are many different kinds of seizure. Mine were considered Myoclonus. Have you ever begun to fall asleep and then jumped or jerked yourself awake? That is considered a form of Myoclonus. That is what was happening to me on an hourly basis but in an elongated format (thirty seconds or more).

After the seizures began to occur regularly it was thought by our family homeopathic chiropractor that the right side of my body was beginning to weaken. I would always turn my head to my right even when I was sleeping. I favored my right side. The family chiropractor recognized this apparent physical weakness and told my Mom and Dad to spin fast while holding me three full rotations clockwise. Were we trying to oppose the effects of high pressure counter-clockwise hurricane systems? Maybe he meant to spin during the hurricanes? The chiropractor said that should help the compromised right side. You have to understand, Mom and Dad would try almost anything to help me, even if it included spinning in circles (possibly during hurricanes?) which invariably made them sick and had no health benefit payoff. The moral of the story being if it doesn't harm your child it may not hurt to try it once.

Currently, our family chiropractors, Dr. Jeremy and Dr. Lori, chuckle at our experience of spinning in circles like a dyslexic hurricane down there in Florida.

Dr. Jeremy relieves me of lingering inner ear pain caused by fluid retention because of small Eustachian tubes. He has the touch of a soft cotton blanket as his hands envelope my cervical base for an upper neck adjustment. The benefits of having a quality experienced chiropractor can make a titanic difference in the length and severity of an ear infection, or digestive blockages. Dr. Lori is magnificent at relieving digestive pain, lower back stiffness, and leg tightness. Mom and Dad have experienced all kinds of doctors in their travels around the world with me, but the spinning chiropractor is still a campfire favorite.

It was time to get some tests done on my genetic makeup. A small amount of blood was drawn from my finger and sent to the laboratory for genetic FISH analysis. The acronym FISH stands for Fluorescence in situ Hybridization. It simply (if I may) maps the genetic information contained in a cell. Not surprisingly, the test revealed that my 2nd chromosome had some micro-deletions in its long arm (q arm) that has affected three genes. Each chromosome has a long arm (q) and a short arm (p). P is for petit. Each human should have 46 chromosomes, twenty three from Mom and twenty three from Dad. Deviations from this makeup will result in mental retardation. The genetics of a human body stores the blueprints of our lives. Our genes tell us what color hair we are to have, how tall we are to be, and what color eyes will be on display to the world. So if the architectural blueprints are incorrect the bodily structure won't operate to its full functionality.

If it wasn't for Mom being as prudent as she is with details we may not have known for a long time after that testing the true results. You see, the neurologist's office called Mom and said the genetic testing proved normal. Mom repudiated the results immediately. After all, I was called somewhat dysmorphic and was having seizures. Mom called the office back and requested a copy of the entire thirty page report to have a read. The sealed report was given to Mom and she left the office. Not able to make it home with the sealed report sitting in the passenger's seat beckoning her opening, Mom pulled to the shoulder of the road to read the report. It is a turning point in a mother's life to read what my mother was about to read.

On page 9 of a 27 page report it said that my genetic makeup was not normal and I did have deletions in my 2nd chromosome. Mom quickly determined that Multi-tasking in the medical world is not a good idea. Mom called the office back to talk to the neurologist. "Could you please turn to page 9 and read back to me the results". "Oh, Mrs. Reger we don't have the results page". "Isn't that the whole idea of the FISH report – the results"! The neurologist overlooked the fact she didn't receive the results page from the medical records department. Mom always was a results oriented person. Mom quickly diverted her rage to thoughts of "now what". What do we do now with a diagnosis of a genetically compromised little girl who is having seizures, is not growing as quickly as she should, is not reaching her milestones, and is keeping mom up all night? There is no manual for a parent to read. At an initial counseling on "what to do next", Dad told Mom in the hallway as he broke down crying that "it may take years and it may take all our money and we may travel to many hospitals, but in the end it will just be us". "It will only be us and we will be exhausted". A prescient statement to make at that time in that hospital not knowing what challenges truly stood in front of his family. Dad didn't cry after that: crying wouldn't help.

The hardest thing a doctor has to do in my estimation is to tell he or she is terminal or the parents that their child is sick with an un-repairable disorder. It is not comprehensible unless your child is the afflicted and you have heard the explanation. The memory of the glib haunting voice and the matter of fact verbal presentation left Dad with the feeling that it was truly up to them.

The neurologist had a chance to brace our family for the extraordinarily painful ride we were all about to endure but she didn't. The matter of fact approach stung Dad and he recoiled from that shock and looked at mom in the hallway and determined that in this most important time in his life he was going to be challenged, and that challenge could only be risen to with his most important teammate, his wife. Many doctors have reported to Mom and Dad much lesser maladies with much greater sensitivity by comparison along the way.

My parents learned a good lesson early on. They learned to be detailed with every part of my care and always question what the Doctors are saying and why they are saying it. Mom was told by a neurologist once "You wouldn't understand. It is a lot of medical terminology". Moms angular response, staring at the Doctor with her piercing blue eyes, was "try me". Some male Doctors just don't realize that Moms are fierce protectors who demand and deserve information and explanations. The female doctors for obvious reasons are more cognizant of whom they are speaking to. Mothers can relate to mothers.

Setting up physical files for paperwork and computer files for research was the first objective. Unfortunately, there was no case history on a child having the exact chromosome abnormality I have. There were a few from a 1970's era medical study that were similar. Medical journals, books, websites, professionals and libraries were consulted. Files for each professional office and hospital were set up. Files for genetics, neurology, pediatrics, social services and early interventions were set up. The paperwork is enough to give you a seizure.

My Dad rankles many who come in contact with me or my care. Mom is the buffer. Mom is the 15 foot wide bunker that swallows up all incoming shrapnel from the procedural zealots of the medical world. She does it to protect others from Dad, not to protect me! There are seasoned medical professionals who cringe at the return sight of Dad and the inevitable two or three part questions. Dad likes statistics and reasoning and interprets the scientific side of my care through his own research. He will ask questions about their medical schooling and who was their favorite teacher and why. Dad doesn't need all the answers, just the *right* answer. After Mom read the report and conclusion on page 9 she commenced digging the bunker to protect that lack of detailed oriented neurologist.

Here is a Quick study on chromosomes. Chromosomes hold the genetic makeup of our bodies. Genetics are the discrete units of inheritance that determine our characteristics. DNA is the genetic instructions used in the development and functioning of all known living organisms. If you didn't have genes you would be a rock!

You probably know that for an organism to grow there needs to be cell division, each cell replicates the DNA in its genome so all the genetic information remains the same between cells. You can see my dilemma if my 2nd chromosome has deletions in it. Every 2nd chromosome in my body will have the same deletions.

Something went wrong from parent to child. In my case, something went wrong and my genetics didn't carry through properly in the earliest stages of my life.

The neurological aspect of my incompleteness is based on my brain's inability to transfer information along my information pathways. A brain has approximately 100 billion neuronal cells and these neurons communicate by passing chemical signals from axons to dendrites at junctions know as synapses. The sending neuron sends a chemical transmitter called glutamate, across the synaptic gap. The receiving neuron responds by firing a tiny jolt of electricity. So you could say that all of our complex thoughts, reactions and emotions of our minds are generated in the brain by these complex networks of electrical signal cascades.

I can tell you most Doctors dread the parent armed with information from the internet. Of course you can believe everything you read on the internet, right? A pediatric neurologist goes to school for 8-12 years to learn the intricacies of the brain. (What science has accurately accumulated up to this point). Said neurologist then is going to field cryptic questions from eager parents who read on the internet how anticonvulsants can stunt mental growth. Neurologists have learned in their schooling the dangers of seizures and how to treat them successfully with anticonvulsants and annual blood testing to make sure organs have not been adversely affected. You can see how this relationship may be a bit dicey.

Implementation of a flexible care plan model based on changing variables requires observation and diligence. Doctors can be patronizing, parents can press with time consuming questions for a very busy overworked office. The result can be flammable if both sides aren't cognizant that ultimately they are working for the child's best interest. Strangely enough Dad always felt better with the Doctor who doesn't know all the answers. Certainty does not make Dad feel good. Certainty raises questions for Dad.

A Doctor who has figured out Dad will tell Dad that he/she doesn't know something when in fact he does. Then comes back in one week and gives Dad the answer he/she would have given him last week.

Dad would ingest (for testing purposes) any new medicine to commiserate with me. He never liked the idea of seizure medicines. Dad realizes they are necessary, but hypothesizes that my body is trying to release (reject) something it doesn't want. Suppressing the seizures may be suppressing an inequity that is looking for separation from my body. The flipside is that during seizures, breathing can be difficult and there is the question of proper organ operation during seizures.

Seizures and prolonged use of medicines (as commercials suggest) can be dangerous each by itself and in combination the one with the other. Finding the optimum balance is a difficult quest. The medical Doctor's front line defense against seizures is anticonvulsants. A Parent's number one job is to protect their children, and a diligent parent is searching for information to support their position of care. It's a results oriented tug of war.

A feeling out process occurs between the family and medical team including dietary habits, home settings, therapy specialists, early intervention programs and other educational needs. The list continues to grow with the advent of new medical procedures such as stem cell treatment, and therapeutic advancements such as communication and mobility devices.

Parents of healthy curiosity research alternative methods of recommended treatment. A lot of times these alternative methods do not speak highly of traditional methods and can have a tendency to promise more than they can deliver. Traditional healthcare providers are wary of alternative methods (generally speaking) of treatment but we as a nation are experiencing a bit of a change as alternative methods (eastern medicine) have become more reliable through better documented experiences that can be shared and researched on the internet by medical providers. Once a proper balance is attained it can be adjusted based on patient response and future needs.

When my parents were researching stem cells in other parts of the world there were many soothsayers telling them of the miracles being performed in their clinic setting. Children were doing things that were medically impossible, so my parents were told. It was easy to weed through the frauds. Why was it easy you ask? Dad loves to joust with fraudulence. Dad keeps emotion out of the decision and was never looking for miracle. We were looking for an option of care that had potential for me and was performed in a sterile environment. Stem cells have a short commercial medical history so a conservative approach was of utmost importance.

Another great example of common sense mental deduction by Mom and Dad was when I was diagnosed with pathological reflux or GERD (Gastro Esophageal Reflux Disease) at three months old by my gastro-intestinal doctor. I was refluxing over two hundred times a day. How is that for heart-burn. My reflux was of the silent variety which meant it didn't always come all the way up. The reflux would seep through my sphincter and into my esophagus. It was very difficult to diagnose and caused an awful burning sensation which is why I had to have an endoscopy. Breastfeeding helped to sooth the pain of GERD, but the constant breastfeeding also created a vicious repetitive cycle because my GERD didn't go away, the burning sensation was masked.

Can you think of a time you felt indigestion? I am certain it was uncomfortable for you. The options for reflux (indigestion) for me were – 1) wait it out (risking permanent damage) 2) medications (risking permanent damage) or 3) alternative medications, which if they did not relieve symptoms would risk permanent damage. What a fun set of choices my parents had to contend with. Jointly, Mom and Dad decided and had success with an alternative healing method of fresh apple juice and other fresh juices. Pharmaceuticals were designed to mask the issue and would have been difficult to stop taking. Doing nothing when your child is in pain doesn't seem like a viable course of (in) action.

Of course with most medical treatments there are long range issues and with varying degrees of side-effects involved. Especially when the side effects are suicidal tendencies as many television and print advertisements suggest. Mom and Dad weighed the issues, measured the apparent pain I was in, consulted with the pediatrician, alternative healer, and the mailman (not really) and set a time frame for me to show improvement before changing direction and trying a different approach. This type of measured and reasoned decision works for my care.

My parents could have claimed long term naivete with my situation. There is *not one* previously documented medical case with the same interstitial chromosome deletions as I have. Try telling that to a new Mom and Dad. In fact, have the new Mom find out this information by reading the requested copy of the genetic report that she paid fifteen cents a sheet for from the Doctor's office that had already read the report and determined that there was no health issue.

Naivete was not an option. Information gathering was the best course of action. Asking many questions of other special needs moms, reading medical journals and plenty of personal observation and detailed record keeping of my day to day neurological pathology was what was required to be able to make informed decisions and have meaningful discussions with the doctors.

I went on a bit of a 60's trip after the introduction, against my parents' well read instincts I might add, to a drug called Phenobarbital. The Dr. prescribed it with the same startling casual-ness as she did at our initial genetic counseling appointment. Mom and Dad were instantly apprehensive. Dad already had strong feelings towards her professional mediocrity.

Phenobarbital is over a hundred years old and is a barbiturate that is non-selective as to what part of the central nervous system it wants to suppress. It is a hypnotic sedative that decreases the activity of neurons. My neuronal activity decreased so much I slept constantly. I missed out on 5 weeks of precious neurological growth without a substantial decrease in seizures. Possibly a 20% reduction in seizures occurred the first week. Not the results we were looking for based on the high risk being taken. Mom's eyes and instincts determined that Phenobarbital was not the proper anti-convulsant for me, nor was it the proper medicine for myoclonic as it turns out. I was still having seizures and was completely wiped out from the medicine. The Dr. was in disagreement with Mom's eyes. We tried a second medicine called trileptal along with the Phenobarbital. Results were negligible at best. The trileptal lasted three weeks.

Seizure medications can have different results on different patients. Some patients can derive benefits from seizure medication that others do not. In regards to my care, when others lectured or scolded Mom and Dad on their parenting skills my somewhat obstinate parents were still able to keep their reasoning and ultimately proved vindicated in their decisions and more importantly their decision making process. I'll take my parents reasoning skills over any pediatric neurologist protocol any day of the week.

Physical development is a key ingredient for self-sufficiency. My physical development has been slow, sometimes reversed, and many times with much anguish. In other words the growth chart is not on an uptrend. I was on the lowest end of the pediatric growth chart for height, weight, and neurological development as grouped with children my age all throughout my youth. My parents learned to preach proportion to the Doctors, not comparison when it came to my growth.

Mom and Dad understand the benefits of healthy eating. Dad understood it so well he opened up two healthy food restaurants right around the time Jeremy was born. Everybody in the family had a smoothie or freshly made vegetable juice named after them. It was such a fun and enterprising idea. My smoothie was "May's Summer Revenge". I don't know the premise behind the naming of my smoothie. Dad may have been in a vengeful angry mood when he decided he would send half the profits of my smoothie to charity. Dad parting with his money is never a pretty sight.

I had to mention Dad's business because food plays a large role in my life, and my diet played a central role in a bizarre hospital situation during Thanksgiving.

Jeremy, Cassie and I all had fresh fruit and vegetable juice bottles that Dad made in a juicer. This practice gave rise to the eventual store openings and the subsequent orange tint to our skin pigment due to the organic carrot juice. Dad took some familial heat for the skin tones, but the precedent was set for Dad's homemade juices and juicing knowledge to take center-stage in the battle for Olivia.

I was in a difficult stage neurologically leading up to Thanksgiving. I was seizing, and not keeping the hospital allocated high caloric pre-packaged baby swill in my stomach. Dad started to bring in homemade green vegetable/apple juice from Dad's restaurant and Mom would feed me. I was able to keep it down. Dad would bring in his fresh juice 3-4 times a day. Mom never left me when I was in the hospital. Not even for a bathroom break down the hall unless Dad was there to watch me in her absence. Dad would bring in a change of clothes, a new book, and her toothbrush. My brother and sister enjoyed fresh squeezed juice when they were six months old, why shouldn't I. The Dr. found this alarmingly unacceptable and harmful to my well-being. The Dr. was steadfast on the hospital swill that made me regurgitate after drinking it. The hospital protocol seems to have gone against the premise of trying to reduce my GERD. Mom was of the persuasion to feed me nutrition that was going to stay fastened to my intestinal walls. It seemed to be a worthwhile concept my mother was proposing.

The Dr. used her professional expertise and experience to determine that we needed to be investigated by the Florida department of Children's Services for malnutrition. The situation was simply imbecilic but necessary to mention in these pages. Our attorney ended the fiasco in a matter of 24 hours so I could return home from the clutches of hospital protocol. We turned that negative situation into something positive. We had a chance to search for a new neurologist who wasn't trying to be so heroic, but one who would do a sound job for a family searching for answers. Our search wasn't going to be limited to the local medical professionals.

Our attorney deserves mentioning. Andy understood both sides and took the simple understanding that it is better to have food in your stomach than not.

Mom and Dad realized that they were to be completely dependent upon themselves and the terrible burden of the freedom of reason and sanity.

There could be no silent retreats or lack of courage. There could only be effort, because my life was worth the life debt they were (are) willing to pay. All of the money, time, effort, tears, pain, and joy my family was to endure for me. I ask you, Isn't that what a family is for?

The Move

Chapter 3

The seemingly endless drive north from South Florida to snowy Buffalo, New York in January was against the flow of seasonal traffic but didn't help make the contentious trip any shorter. My older brother and usually sanguine sister were fighting incessantly about what movie to watch on the portable DVD player which made them dimly aware of the driving infraction Dad had incurred. My cantankerous father couldn't get out of South Florida fast enough until he received a warning from a Palm Beach County sheriff for *allegedly* going too fast in a construction (which is all of Florida) zone. The sheriff looked around the sardine container that disguised itself as our mini-van and noticed my undignified drooling and gave Dad the break he thoroughly deserved after the last six months of disheartening hospital drama. I don't want to excuse people for speeding in a construction zone (except Dad), but at that time I am not sure how much more a man could have taken. After the sheriff returned from his vehicle Dad's semi-graphic undertones subsided as the Sheriff requested Dad should slow down and exercise a bit more caution with his family in the vehicle. There was an inaudible sigh from the front passenger side of the vehicle.

Mom's complexion was snow white at the prospect of moving to Buffalo in January. All else was secondary to her at this moment in time – even me, unapologetically. Mom loves South Florida and the warm tropical breezes that accompany the easy going lifestyle. The strenuous move was set in motion a few months earlier as Dad had made the sovereign financial decision to sell our beloved house with the heated salt cleansed in-ground pool, three car garage, mom's walk in closet (mini apartment) at the height of the South Florida real estate bubble. Mom was not happy about the decision to sell but understood the implications of not accepting the current prices buyers were willing to pay for single family homes. Dad understood that nothing goes up forever (except NY taxes). Dad told me the hardest part about selling his house was not being able to take his three orange trees with him up north. The cultivation and care of his mini grove was an important ingredient to his senility and slaking his thirst after a two hour lawn mowing excursion balancing a sleeping Jeremy on his lap while steering his riding mower with the other. He adored that two hours, and looks back fondly on those Saturday afternoons.

Jeremy and Cassandra thought our trip to Buffalo in January was an extended adventure from the warm weathered confines of South Florida. Cassie had her imaginary pet ferret "cantankerous" follow us from Florida. It made for interesting discussions about Cantankerous' whereabouts as we whistled through the timeworn mountaintops of West Virginia during the sublime hour of five am when the coal miners' trucks were beginning to fire up for another twelve hour day of mining coal deep in the ink black caves of the Blue Ridge Mountains.

Cassie has a particular interest in ferrets and wolves and can recite a staggering amount of information on the social tendencies of wolves. Her disappointment in the federal government's decision to remove wolves from certain parts of Yellowstone Park has left her befuddled with the government's inability to understand the implications of this decision on the food chain. Cassie is an interesting creature to listen to on this long trip. I am sure she thinks this world is all too easy to figure out.

A feeling of being exiled to a cold Siberian plain struck me as we stopped for gas in the West Virginia Mountains. The frigid air filled my warm lungs as the car door opened for a bathroom break. I could feel the color of my face fade to colorless white and my comfortable disposition repine to trembling. I could only wonder what Mom was thinking.

Moving to Buffalo during the snow filled skies of January was not my idea of a good time, but my parents wanted to live closer to our family and we had the tremendous opportunity to finally meet one of the most well-known and respected pediatric neurologists in the field.

The vital family support structure for the next few difficult years of my life was going to be very important for me, Jeremy and Cassandra (well, maybe not so much Cassandra). I calculated that the next few impressionable years of my life would be excruciating for my parents because the energy sapping rigors of my daily needs and the time requirement needed for meaningful research could under-cut my parent's energy level if they could not get a break from my regimen. After all they are only human and humans can't run a marathon at full speed as my parents are attempting to do.

The residents of Western New York can't hide from the numerous and well-chronicled snowy facts of Buffalo's lore, nor do they try. Dad began to frighten Mom about the facts surrounding the blizzard of nineteen seventy-seven when Dad as a youngster used to sled from the rooftops of buried homes.

A badge of honor is unashamedly worn by residents that travel outside of Buffalo. The worldly emblem of the Buffalo Bills is displayed on hats, coats, shirts, pants, socks, and sometimes permanently on other discriminating areas of the body. Onlookers invariably ask, "Buffalo, doesn't it snow there a lot"?

Buffalo has beautifully designed park systems that offer a peaceful summer evening of walking, running, or the corruptive yet relaxing game of golf that Dad has shared with me.

I am sorry but how is golf even relaxing? The preparation of swinging a golf club looks to have many rituals that subsequently have no effect on the quality of the ensuing shot. There seems to be much calculation and many honorable intentions and promises prior to the cursing and golf club abuse that follow many errant shots. The rapid regression of a round of golf seems also to coincide with alcohol consumption. Golf is not life as the hat would lead you to believe. Golf is in its totality, without much deviation, in all matters of practicality, subject to plus or minus ten per-cent mean deviation of results (quantitatively speaking), taking into account separate environmental influences and level of difficulty – *MARRIAGE*.

The October surprise snow storm of 2006 added to the snowy tradition less than a year after our arrival. The storm was in Moms appropriate term a white hurricane. Based on our history of hurricanes we endured in South Florida, a category 4 is easier to deal with than a pummeling wind driven snowstorm. Mom contends I was conceived during a Hurricane after she beat Dad in a scrabble game. Dad says he won the scrabble game or else he wouldn't have been in a good mood. Storms remind me that my brain is hurt, so the conception time frame is accurate by my physiological barometer. Storm systems can wage a tug of war in my two brain hemispheres until one hemisphere claims victory. The eternal debate will rage on who exactly won the scrabble game though.

In the ensuing days of the Buffalo October Snow Storm, Mom understood the importance of a sump pump in the basement and more importantly a backup sump pump. These two important features of a home in the northeast allow for the preservation of tax and business records, photos, and housewares stored in the basement upon moving from Florida. Mom says "So a sump pump brings water into the basement so it can pump the water back out into the sewer system"? Hard to argue with the deft reasoning she implies.

We visited Niagara Falls a few weeks after the storm. Niagara Falls is twenty minutes north of Buffalo and is a beautiful scene to listen to. My most economical visual of Niagara Falls is through my ears. If you are ever able to visit Niagara Falls you would do your underwhelmed senses a favor by subjugating the falling water from Niagara River in the spring time. As the winter ice melts, the thundering river and one hundred and seventy foot falls is as calming as valium (I would know). Thank goodness my cortical blindness mostly allows me to hear this wonder of the world. I wouldn't have known what I was missing. The self-mitigation of natural sounds is as disgraceful as the destruction of words I cannot speak.

After winter, the sun-starved tight knit community begins to plead its case for an early winter hiatus. Beautiful color and sounds return to the ground, people to the cultural festivals, and warmth to the moist air as the grey sun gives way to an unending magnificent blue sky teeming with the sounds of jittery birds. The cold of winter seems a distant memory as I enjoy the slow swinging hammock harnessed between two shade accommodating trees overlooking the lake at Mimi and Grandpas summer home listening to a lethargic giant carp momentarily breaking the water top as it hesitantly moves from one feeding ground to the next. The slight breeze in the treetops allows me to drift off into a palliative state of relaxation as the afternoon shadows creep across my veiled vision. Chipmunks scamper underneath bequeathing territorial rights to the mightier squirrel. The occasional standoff between our dog Sally and Chippy is truly a David vs. Goliath turf war. I am not so sure who the metaphorical David is in this picture though.

The summer house brings me an initial shiver of fear as I retrace my sensory nerve centers for a past commonalty that I can place as a stinging feeling in my eyes on a similarly luminous day in my not too distant past. Suddenly, my memory deceives me. I feel confused, the banter in my brain is erupting please let me fall asleep, I don't want to descend from the sky now! I am happy writing. AH, bliss I feel wonderful as I type this sentence for you. Mom, what is happening, the water is oh so warm now. Can't you reach me Mom? It is difficult to breath. I prefer mom at Mimi's summer home. I am sleepy.

As summer rolls on and the corn stalks rise I know winter is not far off again. The squirrels are heavy in collection. The leaves are crackly underfoot and the windows are closed at nighttime as the air conditioning and overhead fans are slowly replaced by the dusty pressed air of our basement high efficiency furnace. My high efficiency ears are accustomed to recognizing the low density shrill of our furnace when a new air filter is needed. A compilation of basement sounds and ceiling symmetry sometimes affords me the peace of mind to doze off and dream of spring.

Buffalo area residents are never far removed from knowing another person in Buffalo. The six degrees of separation in a conversation of "John knows Jim through Joe" can be had at any initial introduction. Buffalo and Western New York is a beautiful area to be raised in because it is just large enough for autonomy but small enough where you don't have to go it alone during tough times. I do contend that the only tree the October Storm didn't crush under the weight of the snow was the family and friend tree. The centuries old roots were just too deep for some temporary inclement weather to uproot. Far *greater* cities (as measured by populist opinion) have been brought to their proverbial knees by much less. On a return trip to Florida a few years ago, we found ourselves driving through Charlotte, North Carolina. We were the lone vehicle on Interstate ninety-five braving the fiercest of snow storms. The radio non-personality mentioned the city should "expect" an inch or two of snow. The silent eeriness on the roads during the morning rush hour seemed to solicit chaos in the surrounding homes and businesses.

I thought our move to Buffalo was a good idea based on sound reasoning, but damn is it cold here in the winter. Maybe, it won't be the last time we move. I am hoping for a larger family quorum to ensure the votes needed to secure a warmer home address. Of course Buffalo could be our summer home, (Mom has whispered to me as much). Buffalo has much to offer a young family, but it is difficult for me to enjoy six months of the year because of the bone chilling air sweeping off of Lake Erie. Conversely, that same jet stream can be of assistance on those hot muggy summer days when Lake Erie acts as a large air conditioning unit.

Dad grew up in a suburb of Buffalo and many of his family and relatives still reside in the surrounding area. Mom's family is in eastern New York which is a seven hour drive and has proven to be a drive both sides have done frequently. I can sense how large New York City is by Jeremy and Cassie's silence, as they presumably look in wonderment at the skyline while crossing Throgs Neck Bridge. Dad's wonderment lies in the $8 toll to cross *"that god damn bridge"*.

Mom says she sticks out like a sore thumb in Buffalo. She was not built for the mean unforgiving winters or the annual post Lenten bash Dyngus Day held every Monday after Easter to celebrate Polish Pride. Mom was built for warm weather and Cinco de Mayo celebrations. She and warm weather are as comfortable together as New York and high taxes.

Mom is confronted with a new medical system, new cultural sensitivities, new weather patterns, and a sense of regret about moving from the warm confines of South Florida that was not slow to surface.

Mom was built for whatever challenge that confronts her. She has a quiet competitiveness that is spirited, healthy, and adaptable to any situation or surrounding that requires equanimity.

Moms Know Best

Chapter 4

The beautiful thing about mom is that when she kisses me she never has to wipe lipstick off of my face. For as long as I can remember Mom has never worn makeup, primarily because she doesn't need it. My mother's beauty is backed up quite congenially by her brainpower.

Her exemplary intuition and focused brain understand my complexity and conversely my simplicity. She was the first to tell the doctors early on that my stomach is my brain and we need to fix my stomach first. She understands what makes me laugh and what makes me cry. My earliest memory is of dis-comfort. My second earliest memory is my Moms comforting arms.

Mom is asked by many who know her, how she can do as much as she does everyday. Her response is a very simple response: "because it must be done". In reality she gets it done because she endures. Mom's endurance is greater than many and her fears are less than most. Mom has always had endurance to deal with a reticent husband. Mom's fortitude in her professional life has garnered respect from her peers, and she somehow manages a slight residual tenacity for her personal passions. Her mental poise is astounding during chaos and just as astounding during silence.

Dr. D. was our first Dr. visit in Buffalo. She is a neurologist at the Women and Children's Hospital of Buffalo. Dr. D is a caring, warm, highly educated, intelligent, and most importantly highly respected around the country by her peers. She received my bursting from the edges file before our initial visit to acquaint her-self with my history. In giving my mother an initial, "I understand I am a mother too" embrace upon her entrance into the emergency room, she was giving a gesture that conveyed to Mom Dr. D. is here to listen. I noticed Mom's eyes were moist after that long mother to mother embrace. I sensed mom was not quick to release the warm embrace. Dr. D sat comfortably and listened to Mom's experience, as Dr. D's medical students yawn in boredom in the background. The interns made lunch plans for chicken wings over their phones as Mom described the horror of reading the neurologist's report on the side of the road in Florida. They don't make them like they used to, chicken wings that is. Cost Drivers are making it increasingly difficult to find nice plump chicken wings.

The hospital feels warm. Dad's heart is strong as I lie on his left shoulder with him pacing the room. Dr. D had just turned on the faucet to wash her hands before inspecting me. The faucet is running as the cheap fluorescent lighting begins to flicker. Why now, I don't want to embarrass myself. The Church bells have tolled on a wonderful new beginning for us all. A family friendly new city, an exceptionally competent and tender neurologist, and a new me, everything is working out as Dad planned. Don't ruin it insufficient brain, not today! I am fidgeting in Dads arms. False alarm, I feel peaceful, the confusion has subsided. It is 1pm, darkness has invaded the room. Mom! Where are ......

The end result of our first visit with Dr. D. was that Phenobarbital was the incorrect anti-convulsant for myoclonus. After sorting out the medication issue, Dr. D felt secure in our parenting skills to give us an honest diagnosis: take things day to day which felt refreshing for its lack of action and its effect on my sake. The irony of my office visit seizure allowed Dr. D to see first-hand, in what form I was being interrupted. "Theory not contradicting fact", I told you Dr. D. was irrepressibly smart (experience doesn't hurt). We immediately began weaning me from this powerful barbiturate. It was difficult, I had withdrawal effects, and mom slept even less. Dad's worn-out left shoulder received considerable wear and tear. My mind felt more clear when the weaning was complete. Progress is not a word we employ much at our house in regards to my life.

Dr. D embraced mom, listened to mom intently, talked softly, asked many questions, took notes, and did not check her makeup before entering the room. A return visit in three weeks was set-up to mark our impending progress.

A strange occurrence happened during that three week interval. Dr. D called Mom to see how Mom was doing. Mom was dumbfounded that a Dr. would call to see how *Mom* was doing. Calling was not a learned habit of Dr. D: it was innate to her concern.

We began a new anticonvulsant that had immediate positive results on my mental organization. Soon I was limited to febrile seizures, which are seizures manifested by an oncoming illness associated with fever and the soon to be discovered full moon seizures.

Not many people can say they are a luna-tic, how would somebody know if they were? Mom's full moon phone app tells her when I am going to go lunar. Dad looks out the window to determine if I am going to be lunar. Me, I just get hyper and have seizures for no apparent medical reason. The moon does move the oceans, why can't the moon move me.

It has been said (boringly) that a new baby changes everything. It can change one's perspective on life. It can make a good person bad, or it can make a bad person good. Attribute enhancement in the parent's would be my characterization of such an immediate trampling of parental personal space.

A new baby can inspire action or non-action, as in the case of postpartum depression. Sleep deprivation is a common complaint for parents (not mine, maybe silently to each other).

The first few weeks or months of a newborn's life can cause severe sleep deprivation for the parents. When a baby settles into a daily routine of exercise, education, and feeding time, sleep can resume. Can you imagine having sleep deprivation in perpetuity? In other words you are living with the whims of a baby's needs forever and at all hours of the night. Even when mom is sleeping, she is contingency sleeping with one eye open. My mother has mastered the art of sleeping with one eye and one ear open to listen for my brain interruptions. That is what makes her daily accomplishments that much more impressive. She doesn't complain about it, she just does it. There are times I can tell she needs to sleep. I try to oblige her if the dura-matter of my brain lets me. Mom and Dad have taken one night sabbaticals away from home while Mimi and Grandpa absorb the body blows. Even when Mom is away she admits listening for me. You need to look no further than our house for a person who fulfills the requirements of sainthood even though God has not come any nearer to her, or our house. She cares for me as any mother can understand, but she heart-wrenchingly endures for me whereas many mothers would not or could not.

It's a unique relationship, a mom and her daughter. My relationship with Mom isn't of the setting friend play dates and Saturday afternoon department store shopping for the latest back to school, have to have shoe style, lunch box, or book bag. The trauma of watching somnambulant consumers methodically sift through racks of polyester and plastic leaves me disgusted but well aware of why self-improvement/help courses and books are in such high demand. Mom's job for me is being vigilant in searching out resources to add functional value to my life.

Kids love Jarget Stores don't they? I freely admit to have been initially hypnotized by the specter of the social shopping experience. All those whiny kids begging their Moms for plastic toys to blindly deter them from such positive endeavors as playing in some nice clean dirt with their hands and feet. I have concluded that Moms oblige the whining more often than not, unless a Dad (or step dad, if social accuracy is important) is present. Jarget would be a great place for a social experiment. I often wonder if there was a long sought after cure for apathy for sale on the bottom shelf if anyone would ever notice (or care). To gain attention, the sale sign might have to say buy one cure for apathy get one cure for apathy free. I have observed, unconscious shoppers staring in blank fascination at the middle shelf or up. Avid shoppers do not like to strain their eyes and bodies to the bottom shelf. My Mom is willing to pay a different kind of price for my cure and she is smart enough to look on the bottom shelf past all of the highest bidders who supply economically useless crap to the middle shelf (class).

Let's take my last 20 doctors and combine them into one interstellar being of a make–up applying doctor prior to examining room entrance, and working hour, stock quote attentive doctor, and give them a list of 20 questions in reference to me. The questions should relate to diet routine, exercise requirements, effective school material, valuable/worthwhile therapeutic techniques, and pro-active medical needs. My conservative guess is that Dr. "Combo" would get 5-10 questions correct. My father would get 15 correct (He deliberates more). My mother would get all 20 correct and rephrase some questions because they weren't adequately depicting the issue with me. Point here is that a doctor's opinion should be consulted, Dad's respected, and a mother's opinion revered.

After Dr. D. settled upon the proper low dose seizure medication to help organize my neuronal firing capabilities (with much success), our next visit would be to Dr. G.

Dr. G is a (male) gastro intestinal Dr. who works within the same hospital setting as Dr. D. Unfortunately for me, the hospital system did not have the same tangible effect on an accurate quality of diagnosis technique through the accumulation of historical information from an invested mother who has ascertained that the implications of practice through thought and observation are usually (un) vindicated through eventual results. Let's not get ahead of myself though.

One of my great pleasures is eating (as many can relate). It has been well chronicled by people close to me that I love to eat, taste, and feel the food in my mouth. If you feed me I will love you in return. I am not always as complex as the power of my words might imply. Negatively speaking, my size and weight is not a testament to my enjoyment of food. I am underweight as is the case with many children of compromised genetics.

Mom and Dad feel as though I will gain weight when it is physiologically appropriate for my body to gain weight. When my body can handle more weight I will find places to put it. In other words, my proportions are adequate. I am very well nourished with a perfect daily blend of fats, carbohydrates, and proteins. My cellular hydration levels are optimal, and mom adds a very high caloric creamy meal additive once a day to help ensure a modest uptrend in my weight, or at least minimal regression during my periods of hyperactive lunacy.

Our goal with Dr. G was to get some ideas on how I could move my bowels without the need for a daily glycerin suppository. If I could just poop on my own, my neurological organization could improve. We had tried many of the usual doctor recommendations in this arena including many magnesium concoctions. The ensuing intestinal pain I incurred from ingested laxatives wrought "Olivia fury" in our house not seen historically since William the Conqueror conquered England in 1066 at the Battle of Hastings.

Dr. G turned his immediate focus to my low weight to age ratio. This is not an uncommon practice for a medical professional in the gastro-intestinal field, to focus on a prescribed weight to age ratio, that is. This was not part of our intended curriculum with Dr. G, but we listened - Mom is good at listening, Dr. G. is good at pontificating. My pediatrician Dr. H. did not have the same weight to age concerns. Dr. H (female) understood my proportions were in balance, and that I love food. When Dr. G. geometrically turned the conversation upside down to a feeding tube being a necessity for my medical care the Dr./patient/parent relationship became permanently impaired.

There are many children/adults who need feeding tubes for various nutritional and physical reasons. I clearly was not in need of a feeding tube. There was minimal concern with previous medical professionals up until Dr. G, about my small stature.

Dr. G felt as though if I gained weight, most notably in an unstable and unnatural way that it might have helped in my overall development and could possibly help in bowel movements. Mom could not substantiate the bowel movements with the weight gain statement in her research, and she was certainly not enthusiastic about cutting a one inch hole in my stomach to insert a plastic tube so weight gain potions could be pumped into me whenever the green button is pushed (Green for go). Dr. G's proposal was completely counter-intuitive to all of Mom's thoughts on weight gain, bowel movements, and quality of life.

Dr. G said this is what children like me need to have done. Here we go again with stereotypes. Children like me need to have our meridians severed so the tapered end of a plastic tube (made in China) could be inserted into the beveled edge of my intestines to add two hundred more calories to our daily diets. My life of irony could be more humorous if I wasn't subjected to such medical solipsism. A nation of obese children and here I sit (aided of course) on the edge of reverse dietary engineering.

I wonder if Dr. G actually believed what he was saying, or if he would employ the same boring tactical medical protocol for his own injured child who had a rambunctious, time-consuming appetite that would deed away from him a few precious summer tee times at the Country Club. It is unlikely he could fall for his own mealy-mouthed transparent persuasion. Maybe he would have sacrificed his own children at the chivalry of medical protocol, knowing four-thousand dollars was the insurance company coverage for this invasive procedure.

Mom decided upon a proactive approach in dealing with Dr. G. Mom increased my caloric intake by adding another high calorie snack into my daily eating routine during the four weeks leading up to the follow up visit, thinking that this would calm Dr. G's weight gain oration towards us and we could move onto the pressing matter of me pooping. Interestingly, my weight gain could have been measured in milligrams after the snack addition (200 calories). Mom intimated that we were not excited about the prospect of surgical infections, bulky equipment being transported around, and the un-humanly approach to my feedings when it all seemed unnecessary.

Mom decided at our four week follow up visit with Dr. G that we were not very enthusiastic about his obnoxious proposal and that we would continue our search for other applications of practical reasoning without his assistance. Effectively, Mom handed Dr. G a pink slip to end his employment with Olivia Inc. Olivia Inc. is not so much a euphemism as it is the truth. Being cautious of providers in the medical world and alternative world is an important variable in the cost-benefit analysis of proposals of care.

Dr. G. had a pleasant enough office demeanor, but to not agree with his counsel, no matter mom's flawless reasoning, was not to Dr. G's liking. Dr. G infused into the conversation that Children's Family Services would have to be contacted by his office to intervene in this emergency situation. Children's Family Services is the New York State Organization for family intervention when a child is purportedly at risk due to parent negligence. Yep, this is how it went down. Note to Dr. G: don't press a protective, educated, resourceful special needs parent into medical submission unless you are willing to submit a weak professional opinion to a state board, and not be able to withstand tough questions about your practice and diagnosis skill in return.

Mom has at her disposal the quality of being brilliant. She told Dr. G. to please forward the file (at his office expense) to the gastro- intestinal office at the Cleveland Clinic in Cleveland, Ohio in which mom was entrusting my future gastro-intestinal issues/questions too. Prior to the follow-up visit with Dr. G. Mom had sensed the eventual outcome with Dr. G. and had presciently called the Clinic in Cleveland to see if they could get me to poop. That's what this has been all about (lest you forget) so let's call a poop a poop (insert spade if you like).

Dad could gather at a surface level that Dr. G had a nice business of feeding tube surgical procedures and the more profitable aspect of a sterile tube maintenance plan with oil changes every one-thousand miles and we were next on the hit list. We did not hear from Children's Services or Dr. G. at any point in the future, nor did we ever expect to. The Cleveland Clinic G.I. team was spot on with Mom's analysis. Mom and I visit the quality team in Cleveland and the Ronald McDonald House once a year for my checkup.

I suspect Dr. G. employs his usual course of propaganda to influence unsuspecting parents of low weight children to align themselves unsuspectingly with his cash cow of the feeding tube insertion procedure and follow-up maintenance requirements (all of which includes office co-pays). Feeding tubes do save time for parents. My food prep, eating time, and clean up can take an hour. Sometimes the easy way isn't always easier. Being a dissident never was supposed to be easy, but it sure tastes better.

I prefaced this conversation with the fact that feeding tubes are necessary in some instances. I hasten to say that feeding tubes are not medically necessary in all situations though.

Family dinners are our medical checkups. Mom and Dad have a chance to study us and determine how we are progressing physically and mentally during meal times. Our HMO (Home Meal Observations) is better than any health medical delivery system a corporate medical zealot could produce. Our HMO was telling Mom that Dr. G was looking to get paid off by playing to what he thought our eventual weakness was - me.

An unfortunate incident occurred just after our un-pleasantries with Dr. G. Dad had torn his Achilles tendon playing soccer. Soccer is (was) Dad's escape route to euphoria and the camaraderie of competition. I spent some time being pushed around in a clothes basket by Dad because he couldn't walk, and he wasn't going to burden Mom with my transportation needs. Dad is quietly very proud. The clothes basket was quite fun, and it made the trip down the stairs (Dad first) that much more interesting. We had some unremorseful laughs getting down the stairwell (out of Mom's vision and earshot of course).

Dad was still traveling back to Florida on crutches to check in on the smoothie restaurants. They were doing bang-up business but were finally for sale. Dad arrived home on a Friday evening and sat down to spoil me by holding me over his left shoulder. I detected a softer heartbeat. Not the usual robust clock-work I expect from Dad upon returning home to see his wife and children.

A healthy new-born baby boy was welcomed at the neighbors'. Sometimes seeing a new born reduces mom to thinking of having another baby, as is the case with many women. Sometimes seeing a healthy new born reduces Dad to thinking what could have been with me. Dad is tired of traveling and the fact his stores were for sale was exciting but he did consider the stores allegorical children of his.

In any event, even more was thrown on Moms plate because of Dads injury.

I will do my best to remember a poem from an unknown author:

One night a man dreamed he was walking along the beach with the Lord. As scenes of his life flashed before him, he noticed that there were two sets of footprints in the sand. He also noticed at his saddest, lowest times there was but one set of footprints. This bothered the man. He asked the Lord, Did you not promise that if I gave my heart to you you'd be with me all the way? Then why is there but one set of footprints during my most troublesome times? The Lord replied, "My precious child, I love you and I would never forsake you. During those times of trial and suffering, when you see only one set of footprints, it was then I carried you".

In our family, the one set of footprints is my mother's.

To have a sense of Mom's and my travels and pursuit for less physical pain for me is important and would give you a sense of her strong convictions, but the most important thing to take from all of the travel is that she was never afraid. There could have been some unscrupulous people in our lives taking advantage of her pain and my infirmity, but Mom is a New York girl with New York instincts and her frankness shadows her kindness so that newcomers recognize her salvo of questions come from a place of strength and not fear.

Mom and I spent 32 days in multiple hospitals in South Florida early on in my life. Over those 32 days away from Dad and her home she watched as a doctor mistakenly tried to examine my big brother thinking he was the sick one. I could only giggle at the memory. My ethos feels if there was no harm there could be no foul. Mom was anything but giggles. Finding out Jeremy's reflexes were receptive, and his ears, nose and throat were clear of infection afforded Mom the luxury of skipping his next checkup and a large co-payment, but it didn't afford her the luxury of letting go of his hand while I was hospitalized. Not sure how the doctor reconciled the name Olivia when examining a four year old boy.

Mom listened to genetic counselors tell her that there is nothing that can be done (they may be right). She listened to neurologists tell her to medicate me to the point of lethargy, and she listened to people close to her tell her to not be so stubborn and to succumb to the Doctor's wishes (they were wrong). She was never afraid. She was never ashamed of me. The only time Mom was afraid was when the hospital food arrived.

Mom's career revolves around finding suitable employees to fill vacant roles. If I can have a role somewhere outside of my house, my Mom will find it. She will find a suitable role for me where I can express my individuality and creativity. Mom will negotiate my salary and get me the corner office. The first day on the job I will put her picture on my desk. The eventual employer will just have to allow me to wear a bib in high level meetings.

There is a girl who lives in our neighborhood who is my age and always wants to play with me. She is so pretty, and has the curliest head of brown hair. She has a tender soft voice and enjoys pulling an empty red wagon to my house. I imagine she hoped she could pull me in that steel bright red wagon. I so dearly want to touch her hair and let her brush my hair as girlfriends do. I wanted to do it for her not me. I didn't know for sure if she realized I couldn't acknowledge her existence. She was craving my friendship as much as I was hers. I hope she was somewhat aware of my condition; I wouldn't want her to think I was ignorant of her determination. She made an effort to come and see me and for me not to be able to independently reciprocate was dreadful for me. It was a worse feeling than not being able to scratch a late night itch. I have spent hours alone in the night pining to scratch my toe. Sometimes I scratch my head hoping it will move like electricity to my toes and go away. It doesn't go away.

She has since moved away. I will spend a lifetime thinking that I made that girl sad. That itch will never go away when I think of her.

Of all the Doctor visits procedures, hospital stays, and seizures, this is quite possibly the greatest pain for my mother to endure. For now, she has to tolerate her child not being able to engage.

My big sister Cassie understands what I can't give to others, because I can't give it to her. We sleep in the same room and she will tell me in the middle of the night when I am restless that it will be all right. She will secretly read to me at nighttime. Cassie is and will always be an important person in my life; she is my big sister. I want to be the one to say it will be all right to her someday when she needs it. Cassie has more colorful qualities than a summer garden. It is heartening to watch those qualities bloom and grow. She has the biological capacity to lament the death of an ant. She is the steward of her own life and she wouldn't have it any other way.

I was never my mother's defeat. Her acceptance happened earlier than most Moms in similar situations, which allowed for her to deal with the sorrow quickly and decisively. Mom realized I had a right to life and happiness the same as her well children, and any sorrow would interfere with that aspiration.

Mom has done so much, for so much in return (perfect economics of motherhood). The devotion and love Mom has given me is much more than a daughter should ask for.

My father is competent when it comes to my care and rehabilitation. Dad keeps his eyes and ears open at all times. My mother is a mythical figure to me who doesn't listen with her ears: she listens with her brain. My Mom doesn't see with her eyes: she sees with her brain.

Mom doesn't want a parade to be made out of me or her abilities in assisting me in my journey back to the campfire, but I thought it should be said that her determination was never a comeback story. Mom never suffered from the early malaise of emotions or the crippling escapism of prescription drugs that paralyze many parents of a permanently impaired child. Only reason being, she never thought of herself: not once.

Chaos

Chapter 5

Daily routine is important to settle the unsettling effects of chaos in life, but nothing about me is routine except chaos. Here is the scroll crawl of hindrances to normalcy: ear infections, streptococcus, facilitated segments in my thoracic spine, hypotonia, hyper sympathetic nervous system, bronchitis, pneumonia, pink eye, teeth pain (from nighttime grinding), hip dysplasia, constant eye conjunct, food allergies, medicinal allergies, seizures, urinary tract infections, lunar tendencies, feet casts for tendon lengthening, constipation, astigmatism, and you can kick in the common cold for good measure ten-twelve times a year. The obvious omission from this list is any type of mental disorders. I would like to discuss my *future* mental disorders later in my short epoch. Let's give my impending mental disorders some time to manifest.

Trying to contingency plan and problem solve when the main character is a non-verbal young girl with an inferiority complex who feels pain, euphoria, and sadness can be chaotic when stirred shaken and mixed in with two other energetic progeny with youthful needs and lofty ambitions who must be fed and cultivated by two maxed out parents trying to maintain a professional existence, personal attachment, and trying to service their indefatigable intellectual endeavors.

When a sickness strikes me it strikes quick and decisively with a fury and unforgiving veracity of the German Third Reich. World War II documentaries are Dad's occasional choice of television at three am while my brain attempts to return from an interstellar space ride. The television ends up watching him after a while.

This particular morning began with a routine winter cough and a bowl of oatmeal, blueberries, and a chalky fiber additive. After breakfast, Mom bundled me up for the school bus ride like a can of corn to help protect me from the wintry elements. I cannot move a limb when preparing for a trek through the crispy outdoors. Three layers of clothes are the standard for me in the winter.

A typical winter morning would include dad scraping ice and snow from the vehicle window while Mom's car is warmed to a minimally acceptable level above frost bite. Sally our dog enjoying her daily chase of an artfully elusive bunny through the neighborhood. Jeremy continuing his pitiless snowball attacks on an unsuspecting Cassie while Mom is busy slip sliding down the driveway on our walk to the bus. My teeth chatter in frozen laughter while Moms tenuous hold on agility slips away with each snowy step.

It was not an easy day in school, I felt overwhelmingly sleepy and indolent throughout the student bowling competition (teacher aided of course). Upon my return home from school, Dad could see a bit of forever in my glassy eyes and I felt short of breath and a smidgen too warm for Dad's liking. I lay down on the living room floor where the white cathedral ceiling vaults to the sky. The living room ceiling is a reminder to me of the slight acute angle I live at relative to the rest of society.

Jeremy surreptitiously begins playing me some of his self-composed piano music. Jeremy is a sweet, caring, protective, and inquisitive big brother who has talent in piano playing and the trombone. I have perfect pitch. I should know talent when I hear it. He must sense something in me that needs soothing, so he begins to play the piano.

The food processor begins torqueing in the background and it drowns out the sounds of the out of tune piano as Dad prepares a concoction of green melon, walnuts, and my high calorie and protein additive. He likes to tell me what he is making while he begins the arduous but satisfying process of food preparation, feeding, and clean up all the while asking me what my bowling score was. Jiminy Crickets! Why the heck are we bowling in school and not learning how to crawl! I digress.

Am I dreaming? The lights are on, can I be dreaming? I feel a subtle confusion between illusion and reality. Hold me dad. You are my means of rescue, something is wrong! I am ok now. My eyes trace back to the snowy ceiling that is sloped like our snow paved driveway. I see mom on the driveway: she has fallen and is crawling to me up the driveway. Jeremy's music is soft and comforting. My eyes dash back to dad, he is making my…. NO!! I feel….foggy.

Nothing is alive in frosty Buffalo in February except the mechanical snow removal beasts, our overworked furnace, and the silent cellular stalker with the acronym, RSV. I showed all of the symptoms of Respiratory Syncytial Virus (RSV) when we arrived at the hospital later that day. Symptoms include shortness of breath, difficulty breathing, cough, and the always formidable fever, which brought about a cluster of febrile seizures that began while I was sledding down our cathedral ceiling in a wintry fog.

My guess is that the nasty RSV virus decided to infiltrate me and not my brother or sister because RSV looked at me and decided it could extend its winning streak. My disposition to resistance is weak because of my compromised immune system.

Apparently, RSV is making its way through the elementary and middle schools like a big bully, and this RSV bully just stole my gluten free lunch money. At the hospital I am immediately given a fever reducer (which works) and put on oxygen (which helps). Intuitively, mom grabbed my belongings as we left the house, unaware that this was going to be a multi night stay; later that evening she sent dad through the snow covered streets and in heavy winds to get her toothbrush and toothpaste to her.

While at the hospital my oxygen levels have been consistently low even with the help of a respirator. I have been taking an extra anti-seizure medication to help me sleep at night, except that god damn oxygen level reader of mine keeps going off and waking the north wing of the hospital.

Dad arrives back in room 123, and Mom gives him an update (which was brief). Dad is careful to pick me up through the throngs of oxygen wires and saline drip lines circumventing my limp body. Being upright feels good, being on Dad's left shoulder relieves my congested chest and helps me cough out some phlegm. Dad's sinus is stuffy after his mad dash through the crisp night air for Mom's toothbrush. I try to console him by tapping him on his back with my right hand: that toothbrush has been a thorn in his side over the years.

I would think his heart should be pumping harder, after all I know he didn't wait for the elevator, it was crowded tonight in the hospital, and he doesn't like waiting for anything if there are options. Dad is physically strong from doing his daily pull-ups; I am the weak unstable one. I wish I could ask him how he feels. I continue to count 1-2-3 in my head while feeling Dad's heartbeat. I can't locate a clock.

Mom stays with me and Dad makes his way back home to stay with Jeremy and Cassie and give Mimi an update. Mom calls her family in New York to tell them of hers and my whereabouts and why-a-bouts.

Five days later the doctor deemed me strong enough to go home. I am wondering what the weather is like outside as we make our way downstairs through the arterial vein-like hallways of Women and Children's Hospital. Everyone wishes us luck and hugs Mom. The outside world and my own bed at home seem to exist only in my memory. The windows in hospital rooms are small and do not open. Hospitals are stuffy, crowded, infectious, loud, and generally the last place I am interested in for any length of time.

It is unseasonably warm today. Outside is bravely confronting thirty two degrees Fahrenheit according to my first breath of outside air. There is no sign of spring or colorful outlines of marigolds to rest my blurry vision on but I feel some respite from the bitter cold of January as Mom locks me comfortably in our car.

At my follow up pediatric visit the Doctor said to Mom, "I am surprised to see you Olivia". "I didn't think you were going to pull through". Mom was appalled at the un-moderated tone of the statement. Mom didn't think my life was at stake. I would have been at that hospital longer if I ate that boxed and pre-packaged food purchased from some food processing plant incorporated along the New Jersey Turnpike the hospital was attempting to pass off as nutritious. My nose remembers exit 48 on the Jersey Turnpike as being where that food was packaged.

Speaking of New Jersey, after the New York Giants won the Super Bowl and all was well in Moms world, we embarked on our annual migration to Florida for my cranial sacral therapy sessions at the Upledger Institute in Palm Beach Gardens Florida.

Rebecca the therapist at Upledger creates a solace for me that is not duplicated anywhere except Dads shoulder. The gentle touch of her fingers unravels my dysfunction and loosens the vise grip narrowing my cranial nerves. Rebecca leaves me in a congenial state of mental and physical content.

Rebecca facilitates healing in me with the simple healing touch of her fingers. My neurons answer Rebecca's call to action and my brain derives the benefit. My body needs to be pushed and cajoled off of the mountain of residual RSV strife that I find myself on. Once I am off the mountain I have the ability and pleasure to smile for extended amounts of time. When I smile Mom shops, Dad reads, Cassie reads to me, and Jeremy holds me.

My expectations were no different this year. We entered the institute and I recognized the colorful room, soft music, spine adaptation hanging from the ceiling, color coded rubber brain sitting on the counter for visitor educational purposes, and the soft green padded examination table instantly. As I lay down on the summer green table, Rebecca's soothing motherly voice eases me into dreamland as the soft touch of her fingers go to work on my constricted cranium nerves and pressed sacrum. The weighted red- black-colored lady bug blanket eases my autistic mind as I fall asleep. Twenty minutes later I wake as a bead of sweat crosses my brow. My immune system is fully operational again. It is pleasant down here off of the metaphorical mountaintop. Staying here is important for my long-term survival. Upon leaving Upledger, Rebecca asks Dad how he is feeling, what Cassie is reading, if Mom is taking time for herself, and if Jeremy is kicking grass in soccer. She knows us all very well.

The week of cranial sacral sessions in Florida brought much relief to everyone in the family. We were able to visit the over-crowded Animal Kingdom theme park in Orlando and go to the beach for some wave diving (not me of course). Dad's long-time friends the Abbenante's cooked mom her favorite homemade penne a la vodka dish and dad enjoyed a glass of red wine as Mr. Abbenante argued the virtues of the Vatican to Dads open but abstaining religious mind. It was a very nice vacation.

The flight home was quiet; Mom was resentfully thinking of the snow and cold while leaving the palm trees behind, Dad was thinking of Mom who was thinking of the snow and cold, Cassie was wondering why snakes slither, and Jeremy was contemplating what he would do if the plane were to crash. Me, I was thinking of Rebecca at Upledger and when I will need her again. Turns out I would need her real soon.

Mom woke us all on Monday morning and it felt like Mom was talking to me from the other side of nowhere. Mom was trying out my name on me, but there was no response from me. I couldn't. I felt different this morning. Mom bore with me for some time while in search of a warm set of school clothes. Dad made a hot breakfast for us three kids of gluten free waffles, New York maple syrup and blueberries (no maple syrup for me). It didn't interest me to eat or drink. I wasn't interested in being awake. Mom stayed home with me today. Her work flexibility with her employer is great because her employer recognizes how unpredictable and chaotic my life can be.

Mom tried lunch and dinner with me and wasn't able to get my food down, not even applesauce. After not eating the always reliable applesauce my situation looked dire, mom took me into the pediatrician's for an after-hours visit. Diagnosis: bronchitis.

The winter of bronchitis had just begun for me. I had multiple rounds of antibiotics, vitamin C, vitamin D, probiotics, and lying on Dads shoulder to break up the fluid buildup in my lungs. I missed more school than I was able to attend. I missed family functions and could not participate in physical therapy because of the energy sapping faculty of bronchitis.

Bronchitis seems to be the perfect illness. Just when I thought I rid myself of the underhanded bacteria it would re-arm itself and mount another raid on my immune system. The strife of battling bronchitis took everything out of me and replaced it with acceptance. Could I accept bronchitis and lull it into a peaceful state of co-existence and mount my own surprise assault?

Just about the time I decided on hibernation, Cassie decided to add to our chaotic house of horrors. Cassie is (was) a toe walker and it was determined by an orthopedic doctor the she would need casts on her feet to lengthen her Achilles tendons to accommodate her growth. Dad (never one to jump to Dr. Recommendations) tried constant stretching with Cassie and ski boots at first, but the bulky boots were not going to be socially acceptable at school by her classmates or the school principal for that matter. Being socially accepted is not a requirement for Cassie's un-conformist life-style, but Mom wasn't going to allow her to saunter into school with ski boots on. Just as my family has always rallied around me, everybody rallied around Cassie to help her with her physical needs. It was a good time to hibernate while Mom and Dad tended to Cassie.

On New Year's Eve day Dad was tearing his bedroom rug out to make way for an allergy friendly rustic maple wood floor. These types of remodeling adventures test even the strongest of relationships.

Returning home from New Year's Eve Dinner, Dad collapsed on the family room floor, unable to hold his own weight. His thoughts immediately move to me and how he would transport me up and down stairs, to and from vehicles, and simply holding me during my winter of discontent. Mom tells him not to worry about that right now, "let's get you to the hospital", said Mom. *Five* lumbar herniations, was the result of improper bending at the knees during rug removal. Obviously, there is more history to Dads back than his propensity to ignore the proper ergonomics of rug removal. Now what? Three out of five family members are in physical decline with Cassie having the best chance at a full recovery in the shortest amount of time.

Dad's diligence in his back recovery physical therapy plan and Cassie's astuteness to understand the implications of continued toe walking put these two issues to rest in a matter of six weeks.

I woke from my six week slumber and slayed the bronchitis beast with brains instead of brawn.

For now we can say mission accomplished through chaotic family need intervention analysis.

Coming Home
Chapter 6

I enjoy the noisiness and authenticity of a crowd even though I am a reclusive person with a slight inferiority complex. I allow myself to assimilate into a crowd when I am on my father's shoulder. I enjoy observing the social platitudes from that particular height. Dad allows me this temporary indulgence as he bites his lip through searing back pain, because he knows the social benefit I derive. I delight in hearing Mom interact and tell everyone how well she is doing even though she usually slept three hours the previous night. You wouldn't know she slept three hours by her youthful countenance.

Mom's corporate holiday function usually has an over the hill DJ reliving his high school glory days. He also has at his disposal the abused fox-trot otherwise known as the Macarena. "It's Raining Men, halleluiah" always brings the single women's house down. Oh, how the crowds are so easily pleased. The Macarena brings pacification to the undernourished mind. Mom wears her human resources hat and pirouettes with an uncommon grace and style through her corporate Macarena requirements. Mom is amazing at remembering all of the dance steps. Dad never had the compulsion to learn. I would embrace the opportunity with all my heart to Macarena with Mom and Cassie as Dad and Jeremy chortle at our expense. Jeremy probably would Macarena with us if Dad was elsewhere.

It is fun to sense Dad's facial pain at these holiday (let's not offend and say Christmas) parties as the small talk seemingly stifles his brain waves. He always looks as if he has needles stuck in his eyes at social gatherings, especially work related functions. Dad doesn't socialize much at work so it is difficult for him to socialize after work. Dad will never be called pretentious, that's for sure. His friends like him (I think) others find him difficult, I find him to be a worthwhile conversationalist.

A great joy of mine would be to have a glass of red wine with Dad as a normal functioning human and discuss with him why so much is taken for granted by people not guarding against being too comfortable in life. Dad knows he is alive when he catches himself taking something for granted. It makes him angry. Dad doesn't attempt to avoid the benefits of anger when thrust his way. I wonder what it feels like. Taking something for granted, that is.

When we are at an event, I pick out a character in the crowd from the confines of Dads left shoulder who sounds like he might have the qualities to support an intellectual conversation. I pretend to saunter over with my glass of Pinot Noir (Carneros Valley 2008) wine and my fictional (but necessary) arrogance. It is always a "him" in my imagination. An intellectual person is the one individual not speaking to anyone, standing there with a crazy look in his eye. He is thinking about his next chapter to write, the next experiment to attempt, or the impending patent paperwork to complete, and not particularly interested in who was kicked off of the Survivor television program. In fact, he is wondering how they even ended up at such an insignificant gathering of socially inept animals who aren't interested in challenging everyday popular sentiment.

The demonstrative non-stop talkers (NST's) are fun for a short while at a party, but they usually are the odds on favorites for a stupid conversation. They have the gift of gab and are more than likely masking a shortcoming or exaggerating their position in life. When I figure out what NST's are hiding from it is time for me to move on to the next indolent personality to sort out. NST's constantly subterfuge a conversation with a similar (in their mind) plot line that happened to them either some time ago (or maybe recently) that anybody listening worth his own salt doesn't care about. The NST's talk so much they end up with cotton mouth and rarely a hangover. They are talking so much they don't have time to drink water or wine but they look like they are turning water into wine. I once listened to an NST at a..., oops I was almost an NST'er.

The comedians at a party have transitory charm that can engulf a small crowd and keep them temporarily amused (confused), but when the humorist gets long winded and gibberish the once supportive crowd detaches itself to roam for other ear candy and *two* drinks before the open bar closes. One of the free drinks from the open bar is for the spouse who stayed home that evening to watch the weekly episode of Survivor and text message the employed spouse who was voted off the island. The conversations are shockingly transparent and predictable to my ears.

Throughout my social "conversations" Mom has a watchful eye on my mental wherewithal and my physical duplicity as the evening wears on for signs of mental and physical fatigue.

Mom continues her introductions to me with the elegance only my mother can ascend to. Dad complies nicely with Mom's introductions even though his knees begin to weaken as my improperly distributed weight on his left shoulder begins to contort his frame. Dad would rather collapse than allow my initial delicate introduction from a wheelchair. It's his protective nature over my hidden insecurities and not his shame that allow me this rare personal dignity. I even hear pride in his voice and feel sarcasm on his face when the virgin tender-headed interloper asks Dad in baby talk no less, "does she understand", as the questioner turns his head geometrically to study my face. Dad invariably asks "understand what"?

I do wish I could tell people what they do not want to hear. I am able to tell myself some hard truths on a daily basis. I could be a verbal difference maker in the life of someone close to me. I have had many opportunities. Most recently I would have attempted to persuade Dad to continue developing my physical assistant devices he has invested so much energy in. I sense he is feeling I might not garner the benefits. "Dad, somebody will if it is not me"! The equipment is necessary, needed, and requires his innovative mind to complete. It is a work in progress for Dad, like my book is for me.

I have noticed that in any congratulatory or thank you speech, the confidant of the prestigious award winner *was not* the "yes" man in the entourage. "Yes" men are for Dictators of third world nations who are afraid dissent will cost them their life from 25,000 feet above the Indian Ocean. The great consigliore is the one willing to say what others won't, for the benefit of a rising political leader, superstar athlete, brilliant scientist, or Pulitzer Prize winning writer.

The single mother who works three jobs to put food on the table stands above the devoted consigliore in receiving the most praise in a thank you speech. I feel I have that inner sustenance that allows me to say (think) what I feel is driving my conscience of contrarian refinements for the benefit of somebody like my big sister who will end up running the third most powerful political party in our country. Assuming Republicans and Democrats are here to stay. The future political party may or may not be called the party of Wolves, based on Cassandra's love of wolves.

Taking contrarian refinements to the next level would have to include stem cell therapy for my benefit done in Cologne, Germany.

Me, Mom and Dad traveled to a stem cell treatment center in Cologne, Germany for adult stem cell treatment. We went to Germany because I was not a candidate for *experimental* stem cell treatment at any of the research centers in the United States nor was the treatment I was about to receive approved for commercial use in the United States. There are adult stem cell treatment centers in the Caribbean, Scandinavian Europe, China, and South America.

Mom and Dad decided on Germany because the German Medical Community has a longer history of adult stem cell cultivation. The stem cell procedure I was to have is performed in a hospital setting and not a walk-in day clinic as was the case in the Caribbean stem cell centers. Mom and Dad generally felt better about this procedure being performed at the hands of an exacting German Doctor. This *is* to say that we did not feel comfortable with the authenticity of the Caribbean Nations stem cell procedure protocol and the Chinese stem cell treatment centers.

Adult stem cells are otherwise known as somatic stem cells and they differ from the more controversial embryonic stem cells for a few reasons.

Adult stem cells are cells found in tissue located throughout the body. For example, the tissue lining the inside of the mouth has adult stem cells within the tissue. Adult stem cells are used by the body from within the body for regeneration and repair by an injured tissue or organ. Conversely, embryonic stem cells are cultivated from a day's old embryo that will ultimately be destroyed. Herein lies the argument for opponents of embryonic stem cells. An embryo holds these powerful undifferentiated stem cells that have the ability to differentiate into multiple cell types.

An embryonic stem cell infusion would have had to come from cells extracted from an embryo. That would be tricky and include immunosuppressant drugs to help fend off potential rejection of the injected embryonic stem cells. Each organism (body) protects its own protoplasmic integrity by not allowing foreign objects (such as embryonic stem cells) to infiltrate its bodily system without a fight. A perfect blood match would have to be located for an embryonic stem cell treatment to be *even* attempted on me.

The stem cells we are going to use will be taken from my hip bone marrow. The extracted stem cells from my bone marrow will then be cultured overnight in a laboratory to increase the number of stem cells re-injected through my cerebral spinal fluid in my lower back in forty eight hours. Ideally, this reinjection of stem cells will have a positive effect on the weaker parts of my anatomy (namely all of them). My Mom and Dad have really put it on the line for me now. In poker terms I am "All In", as it were.

My parents and I were really excited for the trip. My parents show incredible enthusiasm and apprehension in the same conversation. Dad wishes he could try the treatment first but the cost is really prohibitive in that respect. Dad likes to try all new things before use by me. Dad is my presidential food taste tester.

As I mentioned, Mom and Dad chose Germany over such places as China and the Caribbean because of the conservative and detailed approach to medical research and the stem cell procedure. Dad's heritage is German and he felt very good about the decision to go to X-Cell Center in Germany over other potential choices. Dad felt the German Krankenhaus (hospital) had a stronger sterility than the Asian Hospitals. Safety concerns in the medical process seemed to be the overriding decision clincher. Saying Krankenhaus is just fun, isn't it.

Our mid-summer flight was an eventful nine hour flight that took us through crowded Newark airport and then on to Cologne, Germany. Dad read "Making of the Atomic Bomb" as Mom and I went over the procedural hospital protocol with me a few hundred times. Watching Dad lug my armor plated oversized car seat through an airport onto a commercial plane is never a pretty sight. The ensuing shenanigans is quite comical and can only be described as jaw dropping when Mom and Dad manipulate the seat belt through the back of the car seat as I slide down the adjoining vinyl seat where I was placed as they combine brains and hands to tackle the problem of the car seat being too large for plane seat. The line of people that begins to accumulate all the way back into the terminal begins to relay the reason for the asinine holdup. I imagine the last person in line receives a drastically different reason than what originally set off from ground zero (here to for known as row twelve) such as "some idiot parents cannot get their baby car seat into the plane seat". Some concerned travelers meekly offer assistance as the sweat begins to pour down Dads forehead as his eyes blaze with helpless anger. Mom's exhausted looking face usually ends up being pressed against the window as she attempts to clasp the belt together in the back of the seat while Dad gently balances the car seat at the angle needed for belt connection to occur. The pilot may or may not at that point put in a call to the TSA because of the bedlam occurring in Row twelve seat three. The assembled flight crew gets an update from Dad a few minutes into the engineering extravaganza as Dad turns down pleas for assistance on his behalf. As soon as I hear the roar from the crowd I know we have made seat belt connection and I can be retrieved from the aisle floor. Out of mercy someone should put us on the no fly list.

Some time ago, on a flight to Buffalo from Florida the stewardess called for Jeremy Reger over the intercom. Jeremy, in fear, thought he was in trouble for smuggling a match box car through the metal detector. Note to TSA on the above mentioned item related to matchbox car metal detection. Turns out we were on the wrong connecting flight to Buffalo and we had to unhinge the car seat and race through the terminal with the oversized car seat dangling on Dad's shoulder with Mom towing an overallotment of carry-on luggage and Jeremy crying in repentance over the matchbox car all the way to the proper connecting flight terminal. We all could only laugh as the car/plane seat shenanigans began anew. How we were allowed on the wrong connecting flight to begin with raises a whole new set of TSA effectiveness questions.

Upon arrival in Germany I noticed how clean and organized the airport was as opposed to our connecting airport at Newark, New Jersey. We were in and out of the airport in Cologne with all moms luggage and no delays. All Dad brought to Europe was a carry-on bag with a book and a change of clothes while Mom and I had 4 suitcases for me and her to cover the potential clothes requirements for our five night quest for the perfect cell.

The taxi from the Cologne airport was a BMW and was the cleanest (excluding ambulances) taxi-cab my young blurry eyes have seen. The driver had just informed us that the Cologne soccer team was just promoted to the Bundesliga, so the soccer adoring city was in good spirits. The Bundesliga is the highest professional soccer playing level in Germany.

After a dinner of Bratwurst and German bier for Mom and Dad and chicken, long grain rice, broccoli and filtered water blended to a creamy indulgence for me at the downstairs biergarten, we turned in early that evening to be ready for our early morning appointment. Mom called Jeremy and Cassandra before turning in. They were staying with Mimi and Grandpa at the country house catching toads and roasting marshmallows in the campfire. Or catching marshmallows and roasting toads, my mind escapes me. Cassandra offered her stem cells to me if it could bring us home sooner. Cassie is my big sister idol.

In the morning, over a breakfast of eggs, oatmeal, and strawberries Mom and I listened to Dad attempt to translate the local business paper and candidate Obama's oration about hope and change to an excited overflow audience in Berlin where John Fitzgerald Kennedy (35th U.S. President) famously announced "Ich bin ein Berliner" (I am a German) in 1963. The smell of pork sausage emanating from the kitchen was wonderful as the doors swung the non-kosher scent my way. Oh, how I would like to taste the salt smitten links.

We had contracted with the same BMW driving taxi-cab driver to pick us up in the morning. The BMW engine purrs much differently than our foreign made mini-van. I felt aloft, traveling the city streets to our early morning destination.

The X-cell Center is located on the third floor of a Krankenhaus in a residential neighborhood. I would have expected larger crowds of people in waiting rooms filling out insurance forms and the hospital intercom roaring as ambulances are dispatched after unloading their human cargo every twenty minutes. The resourceful Germans don't seem to be interested in over-running the hospital systems unless absolutely medically necessary.

Mom introduced herself to the other anxious Moms in the waiting room while Dad took care of the payment in the business office. Wouldn't you know it another family from Western New York was in Cologne receiving adult stem cell treatments the same day we were there. The young family from Lockport, New York has a daughter with multiple sclerosis. The young girl from Lockport seemed less disposed to failure than I while listening to her mother's description of her ailments. Another family from Jordan was there to see if stem cells could help their beautiful pre-teen daughter walk after a traumatic brain injury from a car accident.

She had tremendous verbal skills for a twelve year old and did not seem to hold a simulacrum of a grudge on her face.

Dad returned from the business office and whispered confidently to Mom that the business manager incorrectly calculated the exchange rate between the U.S. dollar and the Euro saving Dad twelve hundred dollars. Dad didn't feel the need to point out the manager's mistake to him since the manager was the one with the ten-key calculator. Dad would have paid if they found and proved the error in the ensuing visits. They never did. Dad didn't correlate the business manager's oversight to the medical team's ability to extract stem cells from my left hip bone.

It was our turn to see Dr. E. We methodically walked to the "emergency" room. Dad was carrying me on his shoulder and I was counting one, two, three... Dad's heart tells me he is concerned. I am counting faster than last time. I begin to pat his shoulder to comfort him. The floor is a black and white vinyl checkerboard pattern. The checkerboard reminds me of my play-room back home as the floor jumps into my eyes. I cannot locate a clock.

Mom doesn't like needles so she stands in the hallway outside the room steaming up the port-hole window. Dad had all exits located in his mind (just in case). In case of what, I am not sure. The room was large and the instruments were laid out ready for healing hands. The room felt sterile and the Doctor was dressed in blue with a white mask and blue rubber gloves. The windows were large and the natural light peered through to assist with the procedure as Dads prosecutor type questioning broke the awkward Americans traveling to Germany for questionable stem cell treatment silence.

The drawing out of the stem cells from my hip went quickly and was painless because of the anesthesia. The Doctor was able to draw four vials of bone marrow for over-night cultivation in a laboratory in Dresden with the hopes of collecting two-million or more stem cells. The only effect on me was the anesthesia. As a side-effect, anesthesia has always made me feel panicky like when that first fall frost hits and Mom starts to hyperventilate. I was up all night feeling hyper and panicky while Mom and Dad could not sleep on the slab of slate posing as a mattress. Dad moaned in back pain all night, I was yelling and laughing, and Mom was telling us both to "shut it or else".

We had a sight and sound seeking day the following day because the stem cell cultivation would take forty-eight hours. We decided to sleep walk our way through the belly of Cologne's shopping district along the Rhein River. Mom was posting our journey details on the internet for family members who wanted to follow our travels. I think she wanted to leave a computerized bread crumb trail for her deftly precise marine sniper brother Scott to locate us in the unlikely event we needed to be airlifted out of Germany based on bread crumb co-ordinates, which Scott could handle better than a team of navy seals.

We took the train into the city to see the great cathedral on the shores of the Rhein River, in Cologne. It was the only building standing after the allies bombed Cologne during World War II. The scars on the building remain. I could not locate the ornate ceiling as we entered through the monolith. The echo told me the ceiling was too high for my eyesight. It felt like a very crowded tourist trap we fell into, umm…..attraction. I could hear the jingle of overvalued Euros as the smell of cheap burning wax candles cradled the air along the front arches. The drop of Euros usually preceded the striking of a match, burning sulfur, and the lighting of a candle. This somehow must be related to the value of indulgences.

I imagined a young German family huddled in silence off in the corner as allied bombs drop mercilessly around the cathedral in the year 1945. A speckle of World War II bombing dust has just settled on my nose from a preservation work crew sanding and plastering in the distant halls somewhere near the 8th station of Christ's death march; I sneeze in delayed response. We sat in the Church pews to listen to the surroundings. Could God be found in such a crowd of tourists? Did Jesus' mother desire a wealthy commercial spectacle for her son's intimate legacy? If she didn't, we must all beg immediate forgiveness. A scorn mother's wrath is inconsolable. I cannot find god in the lonely confines of my bed at two in the morning when asking for assistance to reach an itch. Am I to find God here, now? Maybe I would ask for that beautiful young girl with the wonderful voice from Jordan to regain her ability to walk.

Mom's eyes lit up like a neutron star when we finally found her highly sought after destination based on the travel brochures, The Neumarket. Dad and I rested our (his) weary legs at the outdoor biergarten as Mom plodded her way through the avenues of people and shops. She bought souvenirs for everyone except herself. Mom bought Cassie a guinea pig stuffed animal named Aimee and Jeremy a German National Soccer Team sweatshirt.

We began to make our way back as the exhaustion from lack of sleep and travel began to eek its way into our frontal lobe. How can beds be this hard? It is akin to sleeping on a diving board.

After Dad's morning German Newspaper interpretation session in the hotel bistro, we returned to X-Cell by way of the humming BMW. Mom and Dad were chattering a bit more this morning as the day had arrived for stem cell re-injection. Their confidence level had grown with X-cell after the extraction procedure went so smoothly.

Dr. E announced when we entered the emergency room that 1.8 million stem cells had been cultivated in Dresden which was less than the 2 million cells we were aiming for. Dad felt better about the twelve hundred American dollars he saved from exchange translation error upon hearing the stem cell shortfall. Just the same, the procedure was underway. Mom took up her position in the port-hole and Dad resumed his questioning. The Doctor asked me to count from ten backwards when the anesthesia mask began to strangle my cheeks. I imagined myself on Dads shoulder feeling his heartbeat and counted one, two, three....

I woke with what seemed like a hangover about an hour after the procedure ended. I wanted to say four. Mom asked me how I felt, and Dad stood in the background pacing as he observed me. Other than the hangover that went away, nothing felt different. Mom and Dad seemed like they were expecting me to get up and walk out of the hospital. Sorry to disappoint, not today.

The large recovery room windows were open as a light breeze filled the oversized room. The distant voices from the passer-byes below reminded me I was in Cologne, Germany.

I am told the reinjection was quick and without procedural complication. I went through some anesthesia hyperactivity on the slate beds above the noisy biergarten in the hotel that evening. Dad was down in the biergarten attempting to converse with the locals over a pint of German Bier about the stem cell procedure and the potential for Cologne soccer in the upcoming Bundesliga. Mom was posting on the internet pictures and stories about the day's experience as she tried to keep from Cassie her souvenir surprise on the daily phone call. I am beginning to grieve for Cassie's big blue eyes peering into mine and Jeremy's youthful smile as he waits for his front teeth to make their return, and Mimi's apple pie. The apple pie is mine and Mimi's secret.

We had one last visit at X-Cell to check the reinsertion area and to field any further questions or concerns. Mom and Dad would have follow-up paperwork to fill out and send back. Now it was up to Mom and Dad to report signs of progress. I do have a sense of euphoria circulating my veins. It may be just my expectations.

Dad left the fatherland sensing he would like to return someday to travel or maybe live? Mom left thinking of the Nuemarket and the returning home hugs given by her other two children in Buffalo. I left wondering if we could return to Cologne for me to triumphantly walk into X-cell center to display the benefits of adult stem cells.

As we arrived back in Newark for the connecting flight to Buffalo the departure screens were crimson red with delays. Dad's eyes rolled to the back of his head and Mom immediately looked for the nearest sit down restaurant. We received a thirty dollar travel voucher to be used in the airport at our convenience from the airline for our temporary inconvenience. We found a TGIF just before the crowds hit and Dad ordered a burger and fries for Mom and Dad to share and two domestic beers. Mom blended up an apple and some fiber bread in the hallway in front of the men's room sitting on the floor with my blender plugged into the outlet. I giggled throughout my meal thinking of Moms look on her face as she sat in the hallway in a TGIF in the bowels of Newark Airport preparing my food. We all just wanted to go home to our own beds not made of slate but here we are in Newark being stared at by hungry overweight travelers who looked as though they were going to ambush our table if we took any longer to finish an underwhelming meal made outside of a men's room on the floor in Newark airport and a burger that could have walked away on its own recognizance.

As aggravated as we all were I could not stop laughing at our circumstance. An overweight Italian couple waiting in line to sit was breathing heavily on our table when they noticed Mom or Dad hadn't touched their food and the beer was gone. Dad called the over-burdened waitress and gave her the thirty dollar inconvenience travel voucher and told her to keep the change. As we packed up mom's carry-ons and my weighty car seat the Italians launched themselves into our seats before we even vacated the table. As we were exiting, the waitress came back and told dad he owed $8. Dad's already forlorn face grew contorted in confusion. Dad said "No, you keep the $8"? The waitress said "Sir, your bill is $38.55". Mom and I burst out laughing, the waitress missed the joke, Dad looked for the nearest moving plane that he could jump in front of. Dad found what little cool he had left and gave the waitress a $10 bill and a few loose Euro coins from his pocket and let her know that the beer was warm and the burger cold, but the convenience of our inconvenience voucher was just right.

I was so happy to see Jeremy and Cassie, they were a sound for sore ears. To say that they are just as good as it gets is an understatement. Love is not strong enough a word for how I feel about Jeremy and Cassie's continued affection towards me.

Mimi and Grandpa were relieved. Aunt Tammy's dramatic eloquence was on full display, and Uncle Adam didn't even realize we had *left* for Germany. Dad and Mom collapsed in each other's arms onto their feather bed not to be seen for two days.

The treatment center in Cologne closed a few years later, because the European legal loop-hole that allowed the procedures to continue has been closed after a British infant died at the X-Cell hospital center.

How many hospitals would be left open for business if they (state agencies) closed all of the state chartered hospitals in the United States or any other country because of a preventable death? This is not said to make light of a death. It is horrific when an infant dies for any reason. All I can do is report to you the reader about our experience and results, which I fully intend doing.

I have a genetic sequencing break that is not repairable and if I didn't know any better, I would say that the effects of said break seem regressive in nature. There isn't much if any medical technology out there to help me. Adult and Embryonic Stem Cells have proven capacity to heal in many scientific studies. Therapy and schooling is very expensive and so far hasn't shown any tangible results in *my* functioning abilities.

Hospitals really should have more windows, even windows that open. It was infinitely refreshing in the Krankenhaus in Germany. We haven't been to one hospital state side that the windows opened to allow the fresh air in and the dead air out. The fresh air might make patients want to walk and move around.

Fitting In
Chapter 7

What if I could walk, you ask? Would that help with the challenges of dad's back pain, my constipation issues, and allow me a simulacrum of independence from others? Funny you should ask that question.

It has been one month since we returned from Germany and coincidentally my physical skills and mental acuteness have risen dramatically. For example, ich spreche Deutsch (I speak German). It is fun saying ich spreche Deutsch, but really I should be saying ich spreche nichte Deutsch. (I speak no German).

Generally, I was very content when we returned. I was not on the mountaintop of strife nearly as much as I was in the past. I detoxed from my .25 mg of daily anti-seizure medication and even began to move my bowels on my own. The word hallelujah comes to my mind's eye in the relief I/we felt in that daily beautiful occurrence.

A big reason bowel movements were happening was that I was walking. Interested readers, you read me correctly. I was walking with the assistance of Dads fingers as I balanced between his knees while he tried to keep up with my windmill like feet.

The walking began on an unseasonably warm autumn evening when Dad lifted me up from an assisted sitting position and I took it upon myself to start moving my feet in the air, like I was riding a bicycle. My feet and leg air motion was new to me and the gravity free feeling was a rush of sorts. Dad understood the windmill hint and he rested my feet on the ground. I was off running like a wind-up battery powered toy manufactured in China. I took off in an erratic zig-zag fashion headed for the stairwell. I certainly didn't define Newton's first law of motion by moving uniformly straight forward. Dad was yelling for everyone to watch, and I was laughing so loud I made Dad lose his bearings and we were about to take a flyer; face first down the stairs together. Dad scooped me up just before the stairs, and began to yell "You did it Little May! You did it"! Dad kissed me on my cheeks as his long greyish whiskers scratched my jowls. That scruffy payment from Dad never felt so merited.

Our quiet northeastern house erupted in euphoria. Even our sixteen year old cat Boots, who hadn't moved in a year, looked startled at the goings on. I was laughing hysterically. It was a moment in our house that remains as iconic as "One small step for man, one giant step for mankind". Where were you when Olivia walked? A group hug was initiated by Jeremy.

Sounds began to be amplified for me. The kitchen sounded different when we all sat down at dinner for Dad's HMO (Home meal Observation) time. It was as if I had some sort of super hearing. Listening to my own voice was like listening to a field of symphonic crickets during dusk in magnificent summertime.

Imagine yourself lying on the top bunk of a bunk-bed in an old-fashioned tin bunk-house in the country with your face within two feet of a tin roof as a cat chases a squirrel around the tin roof-top on a sublime late summer just before school the school year begins type of morning. Every step the four legged creatures take is intensified by the tin-roof. I felt like I was living under a cat on a hot tin roof chasing a squirrel around every waking moment.

My eyesight was improving, the white veil which I have had since birth, has been lowered from across my blue eyes. I was seeing Moms face and hearing her voice just as I always wanted to. I look like my older sister, something I hope she holds as dear to her heart as I do to mine. I am taking many mental pictures. Maybe my vision will fade back to colorless white as time goes by. I don't ever want to forget Cassie's big blue eyes, and

Jeremy's soft brown hair and bright smile. Maybe my new found mental utility for short-term remembrance shall pass. If it does, I will remember the future I have recently imagined.

I wanted to run more. I wanted to show Dad I could run. He wanted to see me run. The squirrels were becoming so loud now. There is no end to the stairs. Where am I? What is happening? Is that you, Dr. E? How did I get back to Germany? I want to run for Dad, I can't run, the squirrels are too loud. My ears are burning, it is white all around, I need to count one, two…MOM!

The walking phenomenon continued. I had to be careful that I didn't get over-stimulated in my mind and induce a seizure. I was enthralled with walking and everything walking brought to my senses and physiological well-being. The idea that I could do this on my own was intoxicating to me. Moving my bowels without the assistance of a suppository gave me a modest sense of accomplishment in my own right. I hadn't moved my bowels on my own since I was six months old. Walking was the tonic we all thought it could be. It seems that walking was my invitation to physiological freedom.

I suppose the correlation with my improvement is obvious with our return from Germany. My overall economy was improving in other ways. I was easily directing myself from one side of the room to another by rolling. I would steam roll and kick until I ran into an obstacle. I wasn't able to sit up and make my way over obstacles yet, I would have to reset the GPS and find a new route to get to my protracted destination. I was much more vocal especially in the morning before breakfast. I would have liked to holler in audible parlance "can't anybody get an egg and some bacon around here"! I am allergic to eggs they always smell so good though. Also, I became ticklish. Jeremy would tickle me until *he started laughing* so hard he couldn't continue! I enjoyed the books Cassie would read to me. I especially enjoyed the ghost chasing stories about Billy Briggs and Kathy Porter that Dad would make up on the mental fly at bedtime for the three of us. Billy was Dads best friend growing up, and Kathy was his first friend that was a *girl* growing up. I think Dad will always be growing up.

Mom had just landed a nice position with a fantastic not for profit organization almost by accident. She wasn't looking for a position, but she realized the family needed a steady salary and health insurance benefits while Dad was buttoning up his Florida commitments. Money was somewhat tight and my medical bills were piling up. Mom had interviewed for a position without Dads knowledge and was hired to her surprise, and her reaction was "great, now what"?

Dad stayed home with me after having sold the stores in Florida. Dad became my poor man's Mom. Dad and I had some great days and not so great days together as Jeremy and Cassie were back at school.

Cassie enjoys school for the observational value. I am not sure she learns anything relevant for her gigantic future plans during school. She is mostly auto-didactic in regards to her interests. Cassie will read until midnight or later with her flashlight in hand absorbing the contents to her pristine memory. Her primary goal in life is to be a veterinarian with supporting doctoral studies in wolf biology. School seems to be in the way of these goals, but she tolerates it and the nice teachers who supply the protean school material to her rather boringly. Solidarity with adult humans is not in her near term goals unless they offer a bridge of relevant information to her future. Cassie finds her solace in her research and information gathering sessions at the downtown library with Dad and the many internet portals that assist in attaining her research.

Jeremy would like to be a professional soccer playing doctor who can assist in legal casework as an assistant district attorney while inventing a new type of mass transportation to alleviate the world of carbon emissions. No big deal, but he still enjoys his games of hide and go seek with the other decent neighborhood boys. Jeremy operates under the guise of perfect student/perfect future employee persona, but he has an entrepreneurial mind he will soon unearth like a persistent anthropologist.

Dad and I worked on my crawling, walking, and holding items in my fidgety hands. Dad had built for me a stimulation room in the basement where we would spend a lot of time. I would slide down a slide made by Grandpa on my belly to help me to understand the sensation of crawling. The floor in my stimulation room is designed in a checkerboard fashion. The walls have color, patterns, and different shapes that help me to see where the floor ends and the wall begins.

Mom learned these stimulation ideas and techniques at the Institute for the Achievement of Human Potential (IAHP). IAHP is outside of Philadelphia, Pennsylvania on an oak tree lined campus in the town of Wyndmoor in eastern Pennsylvania. Mom went there for a week long course to learn more about the brain and how an injured brain can be regenerated if the proper rehabilitation techniques that IAHP has formulated and tracked for over fifty years are utilized.

IAHP stresses the importance of quality repetition in learning the basics such as crawling, reading and mathematics. Crawling is easily adjoined to a baby who has a well-functioning brain and spends time on his or her belly on a floor. That is what nature has instructed. I do not have a well-brain so it took repetitious crawling patterns to teach my brain how to crawl and move about on the floor. I would rather skip the crawling and go right to walking if the decision was left to me. Walking is independence. Crawling offers a mouth full of dog and cat hair. Walking offers me the opportunity to fit in.

The school I attended before Germany and IAHP was for special needs children like me. I wouldn't call it depressing to arrive at school every morning, but I would have rather been at the dentist getting a root canal. Children with helmets, sad shallow eyes, deformed legs and arms, and cleft lipped insecure children. One thing we all have in common though is potential.

I have had some crazy conversations with my classmates. The adult teachers don't know I call Steven a two timing son-of-a-bitch. Steven has a split personality but he takes the joke in stride with a wink, even though he cannot walk. I yell at Samantha to stop looking at me even though she is looking the other way. She has strabismus in her right eye. Samantha and I laugh about it as she notices me reaching for Michael's remote control to send his stroller flying through the halls (with him in it, of course) when I don't think adults are watching. Henry likes to sing "Oh-Livia our home and native land" instead of the national anthem for Canada, "Oh Canada"! Our teachers are oblivious to our frat house non-sense. We have to have some fun, how many yellow squares and green circles can we pretend to be interested in during one school day.

It may sound bizarre and contradictory but the best chance children like me have to become well are at home with their mothers. That is until we attain a measure of physical independence. This is of course assuming mothers would want to put in the time to repair the traumatic or genetics (in my case) crime. I don't think there would be an argument from even the most successful career oriented moms. It is not such a fantastic idea when a mother is in the wellness equation on a full time basis to expect a greater weighted Bayesian calculated success ratio.

The physical and emotional tools an injured child needs is best taught by caring nurturing mothers who desire a better life for their children. This is not to say that teachers and aides of special needs children do not strive for physical and mental improvement of their students, but it doesn't drive their thoughts and soul as soon as the sun rises and long after the sun has set and all children are tucked in for the evening. Please, do not extrapolate that the majority of special needs teachers and aides do not care. They CARE. The same job can have different meaning for different people. The performance of teachers depends on the tools supplied, education received, and human equity each teacher invests to determine success. For example, let's take a look at the disparity of performance for Catholic Priests and the rock and roll televangelists. Oh, never mind. Sorry, I digressed.

The quick math works like this: one bus driver, one bus aide, one registered nurse on a very expensive modified bus. Let's average the 3 hourly rates to be at $15/hour (maybe this rate is the best the union could do). We can estimate 4 hours a day @ $15 an hour equals $60 in labor a day + gas + mechanical maintenance + insurance + benefits. It would be conservative to call it $200 a day. Remember, taxpayers are paying for these services through Medicaid, state aid, annual art auctions, and state grants.

O.K. let's move into the classroom now. Each class has one homeroom teacher and six aides for the roughly six students in each class. Seven employees per class that we can easily say the gross salary would equal $525 per day. Each employee would gross (as an average mind you) about $75 a day in salary. Now we are at roughly $725 a day for the bus ride and teachers for one class. We will now move on to therapists. Therapists such as speech and vision therapists dually earn their money. Many therapists earn in the range of $40k a year or $150 a day. So a small school will have three therapists which if my math works is equal to $450 a day. A subtotal brings us to $1,175 a day not including benefits, insurance, bus maintenance, utilities, a school nursing staff, maintenance crew, taxes, chief financial officers, and many other daily expenses. I am certain a chief financial officer would conservatively agree with me so far.

I think you understand where this exercise in simple economics is going. What you may not understand from my rambling is that the schools and employees are wonderful human beings who care a great deal, but this is the most expensive babysitting proposition money can buy.

Since my mom understands me better than I understand myself. I don't derive a huge amount of benefit sitting in my chair most of the day learning to bowl, coloring eggs, and listening to Beethoven. I love Beethoven, Mozart, and Franz Peter Schubert, but I get this wonderful music at home and from Uncle Adam's piano endowment. I propose we shut it all down and pay Moms (or Dad, if Mom is working) the chief financial officer salary to stay home and give their children the best chance at rehabilitation. The state would save millions, the children have a better chance of rehabilitation, and a portion of these savings can be used to upgrade the public school curriculums for well children where measurable outcomes can be obtained.

I can work out all of the incidentals for anyone interested in listening.

Being at home with Dad is very beneficial. I would prefer Mom and her motherly tenderness, but my Dad is a fine but distant second choice for now. Dad physically works me out, encourages me with words, talks politics with me, holds me when I am ill, feeds me when I am hungry, walks me outside, and is building my confidence and independence for when he and Mom are not around to support my initiatives. Dad wants me to learn, grow, accurately interpret my surroundings, and live a life of wonderful irony. The irony may be that he is growing at a greater rate than I.

Dad watches over the three of us as we navigate the thorny roads of our lives searching for that elusive seasonal rose. Constant navigation may not allow Jeremy, Cassie, and I to "fit in" popular social circles, but the flipside is our intellectual capacity will never suffer the ramifications of being on idle lost in a crowd of sameness. The happiness Dad envisions for his children is a life-long sense of curiosity and to be a tad bit un-comfortable with our surroundings.

Feeling envy will drive our healthy ambitions and feeling regret once will alleviate the fear of being a loser. There are many ways to alleviate the feelings of being a "loser" and one way is through participation.

My book is my dialogue on the social issues of my day. My book is my thoughts on my surroundings. My book is an attempt to self-pardon my regret. My book verifies my envy towards functioning humans by acknowledging that my participation capabilities are limited and very costly to others. The joy for me is that my book absolves me from being a loser.

Strep throat is a real momentum killer. We happened to be enjoying Thanksgiving dinner at Aunt Tammy's house. Thanksgiving is always my favorite dinner of the year. The warm seasoned food flows endlessly from the depths of the kitchen and I get to cheat with Mimi's pumpkin and apple pie. Mimi's homemade apple pie is without imperfections. Grandpa says grace at the family gatherings to stamp his patriarchal print on the evening's soon to follow wine induced diatribes on work, (ex) spouses, education (including higher), and our many forms of government.

A reminder to me of just how warm family gatherings can be is the fast growing condensation on the windows as the heated political discussions rage. Dad and I sat in the rocking chair after dinner at the back window listening to the evening overtones. Occasionally, deer run through the backyard. Scores of deer are an everyday occurrence this time of year. Drivers take special notice when traveling to watch for deer gingerly crossing the roadways leading their young to a creek-side or a feeding ground.

Dad drew a heart in the window in the condensation and wrote in the heart "May's Window" as we dozed off into a turkey induced coma.

Mom quarantined me to make sure I kept my distance from Molly. My cousin Molly always says hello to me in a most friendly voice. Not this year. Molly had streptococcal bacteria that she unwittingly brought from Charlotte, North Carolina. Mom understood the ramifications of me contracting strep throat ever since my RSV hospitalization.

The Friday after Thanksgiving, Dad and I slept to noon. Dad had four glasses of pinot noir wine while discussing the time-lapsed ecological disaster of placing an ice boom at the mouth of the Niagara River with Uncle Adam, the part-time arborist. Mom worked on her word jumbo in the paper throughout the quiet morning until Dad stumbled down the stairs and mumbled "native" as he schlepped past mom through the kitchen to get a cold glass of tap water. On the way back upstairs he mumbled "panther" while looking over Mom's shoulder, Mom mumbled "asshole" as Dad walked up the creaky half sanded wood stairs. The stairs are one of Dads many halfway completed house projects stuck in "budgetary" constraints.

At noon mom came up to get us out of bed after finishing word jumbo and watching HGTV with Jeremy and Cassandra. We were having leftover turkey sandwiches for lunch. I was feverish and not very hungry. The maternal instincts alert instantly sounded. The look of Molly's face came back to haunt Mom like a low budget horror flick that may or may not include man eating rabid giant slugs overrunning an innocent mid-western town with blond teenage girls resembling Aunt Tammy.

Mom dug the fever-all out from under the almond oil belly-rub and magnesium sulfate in the bath closet. It was too late. I had a violent seizure. Dad had the car warmed up by the time my seizure ended and mom had her boots, hat, and driving gloves on. The pediatrician called ahead to the hospital so we didn't have to wait in the waiting room. If I wait long enough in a hospital waiting room I will contract every sickness brought into the waiting room within ten feet of me along with having to hear Barney sing and dance ad nauseam on the blaring TV with entertained patient mouths agape.

The throat swab confirmed the obvious. The hospital wanted to do a lumbar tap to rule out any other maladies. Mom's incensed glare halted that sequence of events from even approaching step two of the conversation. Mom called Dad on the Friday after Thanksgiving from the hospital to say we were being retained overnight for an IV of fluid and observation and for Dad to bring a book, a change of clothes, and her toothbrush. The only cure for strep throat is rest, and other than Mom, time is the only thing I have on my side to battle this monster. The better constant is Mom and we all know time is absolute.

The eight hundred pound gorilla had entered the room with the precision and stillness of an owl's flight but with much greater force. I had seized violently for multiple days as my built in radiator and fever-all attempted to diffuse malicious and deceitful bodily temperature swings. The saline solution entering my body through the IV was about all my stomach could stand. I regurgitated many times and lost twenty five percent of my body weight over the course of four days.

I can't say that Mom ever left my side while at the hospital. When I woke she was there keeping vigil. When I dozed off her deep blue eyes were my last image. My dire position always left me in the awful un-salutary position of hoping my mother could see the impracticable regenerative powers she implored with her eyes on my soul as she endured the never-ending feeling of the Alaskan midnight sun as the bright lights and monitors jolted any possibility of normal sleep patterns for her.

Occasionally, Dad came barreling through the hospital halls to check in on me. It made me dizzy when Dad picked me up and I let him know by vomiting any remnants of food left in my stomach.

Dad has removed all fear at this point in his life. He is beginning to understand our silent late night (early morning) times together. I am beginning to notice this as he enters the hospital room on a daily basis. His confidence has been transcendentally healthy, even on my third day of hospitalization. Dad's medical credulity was obsolete. Was I misreading his new vinegar as a lack of patience with the medical system and my failure to thrive? I don't think so. Dad has somehow morphed himself into an elite member of a bourgeois society without having the material riches to support such a claim. How many people could claim to experience the richness of a genetically compromised human being? Odds are that most haven't. Dad has found his river of gold, and he is now beginning to flaunt my bold claim.

Dad has reconciled that he cannot be harmed any longer. He has watched his Little May have seizures and not be able to play with the neighborhood girls on their terms. He has heard his Little May cry silently in the night of loneliness. Dad has witnessed his Little May decide whether or not she was going to take her (third person) next breath because of the effects of strep throat and/or RSV. All of his exhorting and all of his love were cast aside at those moments of medical helplessness. It was left up to the will of nature and my own desire to live. I have decided to live three times. I decided to live in utero, during the tumultuous RSV, and during not one but two bouts of strep throat.

Unfortunately for me I had two bouts of strep throat that winter which has cruelly reversed my development to some point two years prior or longer. Four years later as I reminisce, I still think I have strep re-posited somewhere in the depths of my body. I can no longer walk assisted nor move my bowels on my own. Fitting in to societal norms is not something that I think about any longer. Staying different in thought and action will benefit my world greater than the sameness I once envisioned for myself.

The riches of life can be found on the doorsteps of death and the most meaningful stories can be told if you are strong enough to walk away (albeit assisted) from the pain conferring privileges of denying a most imminent death. Le malheur donne des droits. Walking for those few weeks in-between dad's legs gave me the last ounce of strength needed to do battle with strep throat. I hope I can reciprocate the favor to Dad someday by not fitting in to the norms of society.

Family, Religion, and Faith
Chapter 8

My family is a melting pot of opinionated seldom centrist diverse set of bi-polar hare-brained schemers that are mostly normal people.

Let me give you a short description of my closest family members according to the oldest age first. Showing respect to our elders (when they deserve it) is a lost art form.

My great Grandma Gigi (Dad's Grandma) can drive backwards better in her 1989 Ford Taurus at the tender age of eighty-five, than most teenagers can drive forward. She has four children twelve grandchildren, and twenty-four great grandchildren. When the Bills win the Super Bowl she will conveniently die on the spot smiling (not until then though), and we will all applaud her for her job well done.

Pop is Moms father. Pop is our New York Times informational specialist. Pop and Nana supply articles, documentation, holiday care packages like we are all in first year of college in a far off city, and a New York City kind of intuition that differs from most other familial commentary.

Grandma Judy's (Moms Mom) second divorce after twenty years of marriage was difficult but necessary for Grandma Judy to spring from the comfortable yet apathetic corner she was trapped in. Grandma Judy forgot how to do things over the years so she couldn't engage herself to do anything of value. She is slowly making her way out of the corner with the meaningful assistance of herself and the measured encouragement of her daughter.

Dad's physical likeness to Grandpa is striking (as Jeremy's is to Dad), but the mental make-up is less than particular to Grandpa's austerity driven view of life. An accidental work related injury hastened "retirement" for Grandpa. Since "retirement", Grandpa has morphed into a J.D. Salinger recluse type who enjoys reading G.K. Chesterton and Stephen Hawking. How those two authors got mixed together in Grandpa's reading log his God only knows. Grandpa enjoys lurking in the woods on Reger Road at his summer house unseen and unheard from while clearing fallen trees or tending to his garden until a friend or family member needs intelligent conversational support or architectural guidance. Grandpa is the first one offering assistance, sometimes at Mimi's admonishing, but the offer is as rock solid as Moses' Old Testament Ten Commandments coming down off of Mount Sinai. Grandpa only has to be asked once for his assistance and he will be there with his tool belt, searing neck pain, and his golden retriever, Reegs in tow.

Grandma Mimi (Dad's mom) is my secret weapon for sweets, and unfiltered, unadulterated, first rate Mimi love. Mimi is the unofficial hair-dressing mayor of Western New York. Mimi has been cutting hair for one-hundred and thirty years. She holds all the social dirt on area residents that she has accrued from the cozy confines of her beauty parlor chair for use on an as needed basis. "Patients" feel hypnotized sitting in her "hair" chair as information you never intended to reveal comes effortlessly from your mouth. People who don't like her love her. If you have a speeding ticket she will make a call and pay it for you if she can't have it reversed. If your hair didn't turn out the way you wanted, she will charge you double. She can't say no, but sometimes won't say yes. One thing you can count on in your life is Mimi being there when you don't need her, and Mimi being the first one there when you do need motherly intuition.

Aunt Tammy is well, how should I say, Aunt Tammy (picture Pavarotti singing *"Aunt Tammy"* soprano). Uncle Adam has a sense of musical tone that is near pitch perfect, if he only used it for listening more. Uncle Tim is always working but never gets anything done, and Uncle Tim II gets a lot done even though he spends most of his time fishing on his boat off the Jersey Shore.

Uncle Scott has been a paradigm of big brotherly kinship when called upon by Mom after Mom forgave him for rolling her down the street in a garbage can in third grade (Scott reiterates an empty can). Uncle David and Uncle Jeffrey are busy taking over the world let's hope they do.

Dad is not built like Grandpa and Dad is glad for that. Cheap imitations do not sell in our competitive consumer driven double dip recessionary economy (the media keep insisting). Dad and Grandpa did go to the same Catholic High School in South Buffalo (not at the same time - that would be weird). Ostensibly, the same Catholic High School education had an allopathic ending for father and son. Once Dad was out of the easygoing grasp of Mimi and Grandpa and the absolutist aspect of religion had subsided he made the mental note in College to forego religion as a serious inquisitor of his time and moral attention.

Dad's fear for the dark morals of religion was set forth as an altar boy (unmolested) in grade school at Queen of Heaven when in fifth grade he heard from Sister Claudia how first born sons were to be consecrated for the atonement of sins in Egypt and the frightful story of Abraham bringing his first born son Isaac to Mount Moriah for a quality afternoon of flesh incineration and throat gashing with a dull knife (Apparently, Catholicism is not just a slow intellectual death). Dad being the first born son in his house was not keen on these common Old Testament propositions (See exodus 12:29 for more first born son family fun). Dad used to introduce his younger brother, my Uncle Tim as his older brother, just in case. Grandpa was safe - he was the last son born. I can see how this gruesome story would have affected Dad and Grandpa so differently.

This type of looking over your shoulder in fear at such an early age left Dad wondering "WTF". Dad was hoping the Bible would later say "JK", maybe in an updated later version. It doesn't.

If Grandpa and Mimi's God was not there would they be any different? My answer is indefatigably no chance. Reason is a better bargaining chip than mere thoughts of faith. Let me explain. If Pascal feigned his wager to believe in God just as a matter of policy for a permanent placement in the heavens I would wager an honest hedge the other way based on the prodigiousness work ethic of a historically speaking lesser man than Pascal, named Grandpa who being the youngest of nine was offered a unique perspective on human morality in a packed three bedroom house and the benefits of hard work from his mother and father to attain a measure of personal pride that Grandpa utilized to positively shape his life and the lives of those around him. Wagering on the side of Grandpa's formidable daily human effort instead of feigned faith leaves God no decision but to accept a faithless hardworking moral "Grandpa" instead of a God fearing "Grandpa" who exerted less effort in life and relied on the promise of salvation for a large portion of the tally of life's output of labor.

I remember wondering aloud to myself (inaudible musings) if Dad was adopted. I laughed as I caught myself in such a silly mental conversation sitting upon Goose Poop Rock, smack dab in frigid Lake Otseetah in the Adirondack Mountaintops in summertime while visiting Uncle Scott.

Of course, Dad wasn't adopted nor can he be at this point in his financially dependent life. I sensed an Eagle gliding effortlessly over Lake Otseetah slicing through the gravitational pull of earth and disappearing over the swaying tree-tops forever eluding my brief imaginative attempt to duplicate its regal flight. I wondered how and when nature built for my inadequate senses this pristine lake with Goose Poop Rock jutting from the shoreline acting as my immediate personal requiem.

Otseetah's rippled sheen has a small light house on the far shoreline acting as a Shakespearean stage plant. The beautiful mountains build a dark ecological coffin for all of time forward and back to support the composition of Darwin's natural selection process. How can I adjudicate this scenery and my thoughts as having been a divine plan for me to arrive at?

Ben Franklin was quoted as saying that "Lighthouses are more useful than religion". Two hundred and twenty five years later he is still correct.

The natural wonders and thought provoking clout of Otseetah have a purpose for me, and the purpose hasn't been colored by theistic pressures. Once my senses feasted on the surrounding grandiosity of the mountains it occurred to me that our funeral procession through the woods to view the mountains and swim uninhibited would have been more complete with *"funeral in progress"* attachments to our insect shielding hats. My faith tells me we are all on our way to the mountains.

What is there to learn by not questioning our naturally selective emergence from a single eukaryotic cell? Does the thorny explanation of a divine plan work for you? Please don't bestow this incorporeal imagination on me in my school after absorbing the sounds and imagery of Lake Otseetah. I am happy holding my colored squares and circles if the delusions of faith would be the opposing basis for education.

My mental diplomacy doesn't consent so submissively to the Catholic Church's evasive resentment towards information gathering to answer the infinite questions of the cosmos and our improbable existence. Our Universe has determined that some secrets are to great to share, but I sense this is a temporary information gap that should not be haphazardly filled with thoughtless pious answers about an intelligent designer of all time and space. A picture of me would adequately dilute the question of intelligent design.

In our area of the world, a certain NFL Hall of Fame football player named Jim Kelly had a son (Hunter Kelly) who died of Krabbe disease. Krabbe is a rare inherited fatal degenerative nervous system disorder that results in an average life span of two years when diagnosed after birth. Krabbe children (mostly afflicts young children) suffer from a lot of the same symptoms as I. Symptoms include irritability (especially when the Bills lose), unexplained fever, limb stiffness, seizures, feeding difficulties, vomiting, and slowing or reversing of mental and motor development. Some other similar symptoms include muscle weakness, spasticity, deafness, and blindness (In my case cortical blindness).

Jims wife Jill Kelly wrote a book entitled *"Without a Word"* (with Jim's "blessing") on their journey and how their son positively affected their lives and the lives of their family and how religion, the grace of God, and Jesus' suffering two thousand and twelve years ago saved their marriage and ended their son's suffering (presumably, in the afterlife). Most admirably, The Kellys started a foundation to help with in-utero detection of Krabbe and other detectable diseases in the womb (Huntershope.org). Mom and Dad contribute annually to the Hunter's Hope Foundation.

Hunter's Hope Foundation has done more for children in its roughly 10 year existence than the invented Hellenistic Greek and Pagan Roman gods have done in their entire existence.

A simple blood test in utero to detect Krabbe and other potentially fatal diseases can greatly increase survival rates among new born babies. The Hunter's Hope Organization is pressing government officials for universal screening funding for all new born children. Hunter's Hope Foundation has been a beautiful segue for the Kelly family to carry on the memory of their tacit and brave son I would have liked to meet during our brief introduction to Jim, Jill, and their daughters at a book signing for *Without a Word.*

But why would God's creations need universal screening? Supposedly, we are all born in the (blurred) vision of God. God frowns on contraception and abortion. What would a god fearing person do with prenatal information about potentially incurable diseases (not necessarily Krabbe) regardless of what caused the disease or the eventual emotional, physical, or financial outcome of said disease on a single mother let alone the Kellys?

Your health, (reader) is probably swell. My health was recklessly squandered at (mis) conception at no fault of Moms. Would you have wanted me if I was your child? What if you could have chosen abortion based on information supplied prior to birth about me? I am not arguing against new-born screening. I am maintaining that new-born screening goes against the billowing of God's micromanagement and the belief that we were ultimately created in God's eyes; and information that would assail or alter that corrupt management should be kept in check by the discerning religious views of the Catholic Church.

What would my Mom have done if she knew I would have no physical utility, near useless response mechanisms to posed questions, and null neuro receptor danger alerts for self-preservation other than extreme heat and cold? In other words, Mom would be responsible for my physical well-being until one of us is no longer alive. I can tell you unequivocally that my Mom would have protected me at all costs, even her own.

What would your (assuming religious) Mom have done knowing that your life would have no capacity for meaningful adjustment at the dawn of your life? Would she have given you away to the appropriate state agency not willing to accept your human deficiencies? Ask her. Ask your Dad. Then ask why. An answer that sways towards religious servitude is an offensive response, because it fails to deal with the human reality of a new-born child.

Mom was asked early on after my diagnosis what she would have done if she knew I was like I am. Her response was fraught with immediate anger only a wounded mother could conjure that comes from a mother's (human or otherwise) intuition to protect her young at all costs. I have a hard time answering that question for my utilitarian father, I am stumbling with words. Generally, Dad doesn't stumble with words but he might with that question. Ask him off handedly someday if you should see him standing comfortably alone at a social gathering. It's a wonderful "how do you do" conversation.

Where do you stand on hope?

I've surmised that Jim Kelly had a tremendous amount of drive, determination, fight, stamina, and necessary (as opposed to unnecessary) anger prior to his son's arrival. These same traits along with his athletic skill deservedly placed Mr. Kelly in the Pro Football Hall of Fame. Those great character traits may have taken a short term hit (other than anger) with the biting news his young son was terminally ill and had roughly two years to live, but I would certainly consider the argument that faith did not revitalize the Kellys fighting spirit Hunter's eyes eventually did. Eyes are very real motivators for me. For Jesus to be given credit for the Kellys overcoming their sons childhood disease and loss of life seems a bit disingenuous and weak (that being a compliment). Proper credit should be given to the Kellys fighting Irish spirit and their determination to make a difference in their son's name. Maybe their determination isn't separable from religion. I suspect it is.

The next argument for argument's sake would be, religion is good, prayer can't hurt, and if religion helps people to cope with tragedy or even prosperity, what is wrong with that? I say everything is wrong with that because it is a waste of valuable time, money and resources. The young disillusioned men of Muslim faith were praying as they guided the planes of nine-eleven that slammed into the World Trade Centers. Prayer can hurt. Religions are different by name not outcome.

Maybe something good can come from tragedies (acts of forgiveness), but something better comes from no tragedy: the continuation of the experience of life. Don't misinterpret, we all need to make lemonade when dealt lemons, but lemonade doesn't make God real.

Talking to somebody in public who resides on the other side of nowhere can put you in the county jail under psychiatric observation. Let's say, you were to get a response during these personal conversations in Church during a raucous celebration of Jesus' life? Say hello to salvation. If the response from God is when you are mowing the lawn? Say hello to valium.

Religion can have a way of catching you at a low (or high) point in life, as it did for Jim Kelly and could have for my family. The attraction can seem uplifting when an innocent child is involved. Just about anything could feel uplifting at that point, including but not limited to Hot Fudge Sundaes from Route 20 Ice Cream Company on a hot summer night.

Many people believe in strength in numbers. That kind of strength and those kinds of numbers coalescing to a superstitious higher power as the tithes basket circulates lends me to believe that words do speak louder than action. Why must words be in the name of a fabricated religion and not replaced by actionable visits to Route 20 for ice cream sundaes? A hot fudge sundae offers greater salvation for me than groveling for my repentance to an angry egomaniac who decided to flood the earth and destroy its inhabitants all except for a few pairs of animals kept in a wooden ark for forty nights. Nature made some comeback after that heavenly interaction. I wish Mimi was here to take me to uh hmm... clothes shopping.

There are members of my extended family who pray for me. I would like to politely thank them as a group. I am not sure how praying for the afterthought of me makes them feel any better. It certainly doesn't make me feel any better. This is assuming we can all concur that the concept of intercessory miracles is finally obsolete.

Let's examine how circular this revolving door prayer scenario for me really is. I am sick, Aunt and Uncle Prayerpants pray for me to get better, I stay the same or regress based upon therapy, Mom, Dad, rogue bacterial infection, or full moon fever, and not by Aunt and Uncle Prayerpant's glancing Sunday thoughts in regards to my well-being. The redemption seeking Aunt and Uncle squeeze some personal holy constitutional pride from the Sunday (Sabbath) occasion. They have now sinned (pride is a no-no), my metaphorical cross is no less difficult to carry, and God is angered with both of us. All is forgiven during our separate requests for forgiveness (which God hears at the same time as a million other requests fill his in-box, no less) to begin the circle anew. Maybe I am exempt to begin with because Bible reading is not within my realm of abilities. There must be exemptions, the Bible was written three hundred years after Christ's death. You ask for more circular references, how about a quote by Epikouris:

Is God willing to prevent evil, but not able? Then is he impotent. Is he able, but not willing? Then is he malevolent. Is he both able and willing? Whence then is evil?

My annoyance is not directed at something that doesn't exist, but at something that does exist. Married politicians extort wives and children with the religious family values tour during a campaign rally only to be escorted from office after winning a clean race for "alleged" extramarital affairs while web surfing on taxpayer time for extramarital action (See Congressman Chris Lee).

Televangelists and mega church preachers crusading against the "immorality" of homosexuality should be writing in advance an apology and resignation letter for drug-induced homosexual fornication to Ted Haggard's shocked and un-believing congregation; but parishioners will believe their savior was born of a virgin mother, died, rose from the dead and ascended into the clouds for life ever-after in a state of bliss where believers will be with him upon death. The resignation letter may or may not blame pride as the reason for hiding such an evil transgression. Not the fact he is a closet homosexual and lied about it to his wife, children, congregation, and self. Mr. Preacher, don't be ashamed you were intelligently designed lest you forget. You just made un-intelligent decisions based on your free will. Hard to get past the contradictions, but let's continue.

Being an un-confrontational person I can't get the Islamic religion to pass logical muster for my personal use either:

"Truly Allah loves those who fight in his cause in battle array, as if they were a solid cemented structure" Surah 61, The Qur'an.

That is a strong (maybe extremist) statement of belief and faith. Not too much different than the many books in the Old Testament. In the absence of religious belief would there have been a nine-eleven? In the absence of faith there would have been no glorious paradise full of virgins for the martyrs of Islamic faith to ascend to. Is anyone praying for the virgins?

Continuing to point out obvious contradictions in religion is not very appealing to me because of the obviousness of it and other books can describe the contradictions better, like the Bible or the Qur'an. My purpose was to show you it can be more worthwhile without having to answer to external supervisors in the sky, rather only answering to your own internal supervisor like my Grandpa does.

As an amateur philosopher I have traveled on my tangent train of family, religion, and faith long enough. I have made no mistakes in life to learn from, and I am free of sin, but not by choice. The subtlety here is that an intelligent designer made the mistake that I am unable to make mistakes which, makes his son that he sent here to forgive me of my sins obsolete. I am now left to clean up the mess with *my family, my religion, and my faith*. Not anybody else's.

Going Away
Chapter 9

In hindsight the gradual separation of family members moving on as they grow older is completely transparent. Work, travel, new families, and pure distance enhance the divide. I see it as separation through ascension, if you will. I will not have any social ascension to account for in my lifetime so I live vicariously through Jeremy and Cassandra's consistently rapid ascent to their bright professional futures and unique personal conquests. Like the time Jeremy was going to get his black belt "no matter what". I spent a few afternoons in the packed dojo watching chubby kids attempting back kicks. I pictured myself out on the mats taking out a few of the boys with leg sweeps. Suffice it to say, the only black belt Jeremy wears is when he has picture day in school.

My social standing will never be based on the acquisition of friends, assets, or if I am living a full enough life, enemies. My individual social achievement will have been that I was alive. That is it. I was here. Will it have mattered to this world that I was here, I doubt it. I am not too much different than 99.99% of the masses in that respect. The people who have made the difference are the ones who have affected change, left a legacy, found a cure, dared to think conceptually, or entertained the masses. Other than my brief stint walking my entertainment value plummeted like Obama's approval ratings.

What will matter to me when I am older will be the same customary matters of living that are important to me now. My physical survival depends on my mother feeding me. Not biting the hand that feeds me is my reality. My mental enrichment depends on my observation ability, and conversations with dad. The sameness of my everyday needs should have been prefaced by stating when I am healthy. Just like you, my needs change when I am ill, only a bit more drastically for me. I am rather low maintenance when healthy. No Jersey girl here.

I won't ever need a new pair of earrings to impress a certain boy, a new car for college, a wedding dress, or my first baby shower party with all of my friends and family. I certainly will never need to wait for the cable guy between the hours of 10 and 4 at my own house that the bank owns or answer a random phone call asking for my opinion on the adequacy of our nation's political leaders. I would be more than happy to offer responses outside of the multiple choices pre-arranged for my leisurely mental disposal that surely would make it into the polling results under the "other" heading.

I am growing accustomed to watching everyone grow up and old around me while I stay still. My scenery doesn't change as much as I would like so I have to rely on my imaginative prowess to endow my senses so I can keep afloat of the current event conversations during future family dinner gatherings.

I have been growing fearful of an impending loneliness when my brother and sister are gone and Mom and Dad are older, but the distance will allow me to detect the jumps in physical and intellectual growth upon their return to wherever home may be. I have recognized the subtle growth shifts in our house to this point. The development is enjoyable to observe and I am grateful for being born into a family with such distinctive contrasting dispositions.

My brother and sister are beginning to speak of college and boyfriends/girlfriends. Jeremy won't admit very much on the girl part though. I just can't reconcile the speed of time. I try to value the future based on a longer time-frame than my own existence and it is a wonderful future to imagine. The clothing turn-over in the closet of my sister keeps me informed of the upcoming seasons and wardrobe style changes. I defer to her acute fashion sense since I wear the hand me down clothes and shoes. I prefer the worn look.

Boots our old black fur (why doesn't it turn grey?) and white pawed cat has seen a lot in her eighteen years. She was the only one of our immediate family around when Mom and Dad were married twelve years ago. Boots has enjoyed the serendipity of her last few years. Boots knew it was her hour when it was her hour. She purred less and scoffed at the idea of play on her arthritic hips. Boot's eyes had lost their full moon feature a few years back. Her faculties were administered much less accurately much to the consternation of Dad. Dad ended up buying a covered litter box way late in the game. Boots felt awful about becoming such a liability in our house but the local community derided the idea of an old cats low income home for old cats on social security and medicare. The local yokels didn't want the value of their middle income neighborhoods to deteriorate in value with the Boots riffraff type being huddled into an old cats home with daily senior cat vans escorting them to the veterinarian. So the well-informed readers of middle "American Idol" sensibilities picketed and paraded their fears up and down Main Street predicting anarchy in the hood along with higher taxes and over-worked policemen and firemen not able to do their jobs until the politicians gave in for fear of losing cushy jobs with a stocked pension and premium health insurance coverage in the next election. It was officially decided, no old cats home for Boots in our warm and hospitable community. When Dad took boots to the veterinarian that last day all I could feel was as I said goodbye to Boots, it would be my turn soon. Not to be put asleep! To be taken to a "home" away from my beloved family.

Residential Mental Hygiene Facilities are homes for people like me in the unstable New York State operated and licensed homes for the disabled. Recently, Mom and Dad were discussing a New York Times article (furnished by Pop of course) relating to the number of unpunished appalling crimes committed at the hands of union workers (often repeat offenders) who tend to "consumers" like me. Mom and Dad have always contended they would never put me in a Residential Mental Hygiene Facility or other state agency equivalent. The horrific details of alleged wide spread physical abuse and ignominy at the hands of some dreadful employees left Dad seething in anger over the hideousness of the crimes and the utter indifference and complicity of the state union that in turn negotiates a transfer of the "alleged" guilty employees to other facilities after temporary leaves of absences.

The cowardice to surreptitiously impose an evil will on a human being as feeble as myself is worthy of more than just meaningless reprimands and transfers to other unsuspecting residences. At the minimum it is worthy of local police investigations.

Watching my door everyday in fear of who may enter to deliver my daily punishment instead of Mom walking through my door with her warm smile and morning encouragement is a scary thought. It is a thought I have always considered. I have tried not to tell fibs to myself about my future. Dad's back surgery was successful enough where he doesn't need my gangly body re-injuring it because of his insistence to hold my self-respect at the eye level of others and not from the low angle of a wheelchair.

The perfect crime in life is guilt. Guilt is born internally and if you are not protected and shielded from its harms it can eat away at your personal self worth. Just because state employees are not found guilty by a court of law doesn't mean they shouldn't feel immense guilt for their actions. It leads me to believe that the moral standards are palpably low in the management ranks at the New York State Commission on Quality of Care and Advocacy for Persons with Disabilities. A favorite union motto is that unions protect working families. Or harm working families, if you were to ask me. The Civil Service Employees Association of New York protects their dues (members) quite ferociously.

Non-verbal victims make it difficult to arbitrate with equanimity as it seems union employees have taken the stance that they are the victims. Who stays in that type of abusive relationship willingly? How is it possible I am holding more harmful guilt over my future living arrangements than the vile people who repeatedly are put in positions to harm the defenseless?

Dad always tells us it's how hard you hit back not how hard you have been hit. It's no secret Dad is a fan of the epic Rocky motion pictures. Jeremy gets the "hit back" or the "you only get one shot in life" speech on the way to soccer. Fear can stoke anger which then prompts action, or fear makes you shrink and hide until the inevitable occurs: nothing. I have always been curious about my father's real fear level. He fears nothing. So he says. If I could ever ask one question to my father it would be "what do you fear Dad". He cannot hide the truth from me to protect what he supposes he is thought of by me. I know what Dad fears. Dad fears letting me go. Dad fears guilt. He is lying if he says otherwise.

When somebody says to Dad "You sacrifice so much for the sake of your daughter" Dad responds "How do you mean"? The questioner says because you don't sleep, eat, and you live your life on the verge of an emergency room visit. Dad says that is not sacrifice: "sacrifice would be if I did all those fun things you are implying instead of my daughter's needs"? Sacrifice is surrendering the **greater** of two or more competing pleasures for the benefit of the other. I am watching for signs when I am the other side of the sacrifice equation.

Good parents do give up their prior freedoms when children arrive. How long should parents be liable, and at what price? Moms are willing to lay down their lives. Dads, well a few hundred bucks here and there leaves them feeling like a martyr. College age seems a fair cutoff, or if you are my sister Cassandra the eighth grade seems more likely.

Couldn't I live in a nice comfortable home with state paid employees giving me a daily suppository, toughing out the occasional seizure with me, washing my hair five times a week, and reading to me intellectually compelling books (stretching it there) without feeling like I am missing out on something? Mom and Dad can pick me up on weekends after Jeremy and Cassandra are off at college, and bring me home for certain holidays and birthdays. In between, Mom and Dad can enjoy quiet dinners, trips to the tropics, and spend some time reading "Somatic Cell Nuclear Transfer Techniques for Dummies" without slumbering off after two paragraphs because of substantial sleep deprivation.

I am afraid of the eventual transfer of my living arrangements, not for my sake but my parents. They will have to get their lives back at a later date when Jeremy and Cassandra have moved on. My own version of going off to college awaits the three of us. My college just won't be labeled an institute for higher learning.

I have died many times since my first birthday. Death has never been repressed in my mind. I can't repress something so close to me. I have not died in the literal sense only the metaphorical sense. At a young age death became a part of my life. Crossing the threshold into a hospital emergency room is a humbling experience that enhances the spectacular oddity that we even exist on earth. My body's irrational persistence to heal leaves me humbled. I have known death in my dreams during health scares.

It does not scare me to think I may know death before my parents death. It relieves me to know my Dad's singular fear will subside upon my death. He probably would attain some measure of immortality if I were to live to an old age. He couldn't pass on knowing I was left behind in a Residential Mental Hygiene Facility. I would be fine with the name "Disabled Living Home". Mental Hygiene Facility? I don't want my brain flossed and scrubbed with a toothbrush.

It relieves me to know that I will know for sure the great secret of the afterlife before my family. It relieves me to know that I won't even know when I am dying. Death is reflective and conceptual. My parents have been told by neurologists in Cleveland, New York, Philadelphia, Miami, West Palm Beach, and Buffalo I am neither reflective nor conceptual. If this is the case I cannot fear death. Let's keep my conceptual powers a secret to these pages. Most neurologists are too egotistical to hear that they were wrong about a patient.

I have had reoccurring dreams of staggering conceptualization where I have conversations with other family members. It is a startling dream, a realistic dream, a passionate dream for an unfeasible conscious aspiration. During times of personal melancholy a pattern has arisen in me where a sphere of my brain becomes more active when I am asleep. My austere disappointments in life have a way of manifesting themselves into my sub-consciousness when I am asleep.

Have you had the dream where you cannot run from a deranged stalker? Have you had the dream where you are trying to talk coherently but you cannot? For me, those are not dreams. That is my daily life. I am living in reverse order from bad dreams to a healthy person's reality. The ridiculousness of the dreams is that they are so vivid.

I have raised my father to understand that my clandestine internal struggles to understand my own obvious lack of social relevance and personal struggles to walk and talk have been more about his character education than mine. It is innate for me to attempt to overcome my own struggles, but it never was a forgone conclusion that because he is my father he would automatically identify with my internal strife while simultaneously dealing with his own. His pride grows as I regress, his quiet understanding reflects his true empathy for me, and his inner strife is his currency for the impracticable privilege of communicating with his un-salutary youngest daughter.

I suppose we all think of the possibility of our own death after the age of seven. If I could imagine my death I suppose it would go down like this:

Dad has a sympathy seizure in his dream one evening. The magnitude of the sub-conscious facial contortions and physical hemorrhaging wakes him from his sleep. I could faintly hear his voice as he stumbles out of bed into my room to check on my blankets to make sure I am covered. The physical duress of his dream brings extra warmth into my room. His shadow is looming over me as his voice although whispering seems to boom in my ears. The crescent moon peeked through the window over Dads shoulder like a sickle. Dad yells for mom.

A violent seizure strikes me while Dad is in my room. The irony is too unsettling for dad's liking. My temperature is 104 by Dads calculation and my forehead could be used to iron clothes. The Celsius to Fahrenheit always throws Mom, so Dad handles the degree conversion. After grabbing her toothbrush from the bath Mom whisks me to the hospital at four am on a Saturday morning. Our car feels warm even with the air cooler on. I withstand three large seizures in the car as Mom avoids rather matter-of-factly a falling umbrageous oak tree during our pre-dawn race to the emergency room. Being febrile is dangerous because if the fever is severe enough it could bring the seizures like rain. It was a driving rain this morning inside our car and out.

I have just become an interesting person to every member of the emergency room team. Happy hour, two for one if you will.

The systematic deduction of common maladies begins with a review of my recent history with Mom and the doctors. The standard work orders for a lumbar puncture and blood work to assess a possible viral infection are quickly put in motion. Mom relates the story of my recent gastrointestinal workup at the imaging center the day before which included injecting a dark dye contrast into my bowels for evidence review by a gastrointestinal doctor for potential structural deficiencies.

I begin receiving measured doses of fever reducers and anti-convulsants, but the seizures persist through to sunlight. Dad arrives in the morning after leaving Jeremy and Cassie in charge of themselves at the house. Jeremy asks Dad to give me a hug for him, so he does upon arrival.

It takes a few hours to relieve the status epileptic. If you were to ring me out like an old rag, narcotics and fever reducer would flush through my skin.

The morning attending nurse begins to ask questions for the computerized chart system. Height, weight, age, date of birth, and religious affiliation. Dad's head swings one-hundred and eighty degrees, he interrupts Mom to answer, "Democrat". The nurse asked if we were religious, Dad pronounced "Hell No, we are atheist". Mom begins to dig the bunker for her own protection this time. If the quality of care were to drop because of our religious non-beliefs we would have converted to agnosticism to appease. Something about the word atheist scares people. Then it occurs to me in-between seizures that I never needed a religious affiliation. Faith is not useful for moral reasoning for me, it is not useful for inspiration, and it is not useful for consolation. Faith is not useful in understanding the basic foundations of life or the universe for a child.

I am moved up to the pediatric intensive care unit (PICU) after the seizures subsided after some heavy narcotics and sedatives. Of course I was given a window that doesn't open in my room. Dad belatedly asks why the windows don't open in Western Hospitals. "Bugs would get in". Dad is not interested in offering up the idea of screens to the board of directors.

I am able to faintly recognize Mom seven hours later for a brief blurry moment. Status epileptic is not a phrase I have heard before in my life. I begin to seize regularly now when awake. I should have known it was serious by our four a.m. race through the streets. This is not my idea of quality time with Mom. I was able to steal a brief look from Mom's forlorn always makeup free face. Her face succinctly summarizes my current state. Somehow I have to awaken my "A" game for this new opponent. I am picturing Jeremy listening to rap music to gather his anger before a big soccer game. I am not focused, I am in pain, I am seizing, and I feel an internal dilemma brewing in my soul. Has my soul arrived in time to help me or has its arrival been planned for this moment? Soul, where have you been? It feels that something tangible has arrived. Is it the power of the serene moment or have I been duped into a peaceful cloud of imminent expiry.

Dad's battle armor has been fitted with his political annotation to the religious inquiry from the interrogating hospital nurse. Mom has her bunker digging shovels on ready, and Mimi had Jeremy and Cassandra on full distraction alert. The rest is up to me.

All tests begin to come back negative but the fever is as persistent as a landlord who is owed past due rent. Dad tells mom the PICU waiting room is named after (in memory of) a two year old girl. I wish Dad could be a little less aware of his surroundings so the intensity of the situation might decrease.

This damn fever keeps hounding me. Further tests are negative. The only time I feel no pain is when I am asleep. Sleeping for eternity feels like a nice option right now. I probably could sleep for eternity but it would really piss Dad off. I was sleeping forever before I was born so what could the difference really be at this point? The love can continue as the memory of me becomes distant. I am in so much pain. The tubes in my throat are helping me breathe, the tube in my nose is extracting bile from the trapped contrast from the gastrointestinal procedure, and the needle in my wrist is injecting medicine and withdrawing blood my body desperately needs at the whim of a semi-focused attending doctor's request.

Dad's back and Mom's heart are taking equal parts beating and pacing at my bedside. My regression feels almost complete to me but my parent's denial marches on. The pain in my head is searing, my throat is burning and my body is numb. Boots was put to rest why not me.

I don't owe any apologies and none are owed to me. This middle world I inhabit isn't for me any longer. My infirmary needs are too great. "Mom, I wouldn't have been mad if you decided otherwise prior to my birth, I promise I wouldn't have been mad"! How could I be, I sense your un-consolable anguish. Have I brought anything to the table of life for you other than worry?

It's funny, I am not afraid to die and I don't believe in the afterlife. I am not going to a better place, I am not going anywhere. My father's shoulder will not be needed there, I need his shoulder now. The outer reaches of my lungs are crackling as I breathe. I am strapped to many machines Dad cannot get to me.

When my eyes are closed I only feel Moms pain but I know I don't want them open again. I want the easy way out. I just want out now. It is my hour, it is my time.

Death has a way of expanding life's accomplishments and bolstering reputations such as a great artist's masterpiece. I have no accomplishments. I have no reputation. I have nothing except the desire for infinite sleep.

My body cannot stand the heat. I am cold at the same time. Ice towels are laid across my chest I convulse with the conflict. I turn my head towards the window to feel the sun on my face like when Dad's sunroof was open going to Grandpa's country house in the summertime. I hear seagulls off in the distance. They are angry for food. The sun is setting my room is quiet. Damn those seagulls are loud. I am small and weak. The world is not made for someone like me. Small things on earth die off quicker.

Waves of seizures are rolling in, but I am coherent. I only hear seagulls and see Mom. There is no ceiling, there is no clock, and I feel no floor. The seagulls are hungry but it is quiet in my room. Mom feels tired. The honors of age have bestowed great beauty on her. I hear her breathing.

The doctors are helpless. There will be no chaplain. I have nothing to atone for. Dad cannot help, he is an angry bystander. He need not be angry now, it is avoidable. Be accepting Dad, let me see you smile, you should smile. I am.

Oh to see Jeremy's warm face one more time. He is a happy, emphatically smart, enterprising young man who always thought about my comfort. I am smiling.

How I would embrace Cassandra right now. We could feed the hungry seagulls together. She would know just what to feed them. I could see her run through them as they settle onto the bread crumbs. She is my big sister. I am smiling.

I hear the Seagulls as we stroll along the Outer Banks. I feel the warm sun as we sit on Spider Rocks in the harbor watching the sailboats tame the wind and crease the water.

Even Rebecca cannot get me down from this mountain. The seagulls are moving closer, the room is spiraling. Mom tells me she loves me. The seizures are inside and I cannot get them out to release what is ailing me. I haven't eaten in days but my stomach is uncomfortably bloated. Damn seagulls are in my room following the bread trail. The window is closed how did they get in? Mom has a tear. Smile Mom, I am smiling.

Dad's only consolation now was his continual effort. He understands my pain as he looks in my eyes. Dad has listened to me all these years. He has come so far. I am smiling.

Mom asks the Doctor an exuberant "what if" question. The doctor shakes his head Mom turns back to me sobbing. Don't cry Mom, can't you see my smile? That seizure felt different. The drugs are of no use. I see "May's Window" outlined in a heart across my hospital window. I am smiling. I smell Mimi's apple pie. I feel Mom's breath. I see a shiny white dove amongst the seagulls. I was never meant to be heard, so I whisper towards Dad "no more fear Dad". I am smiling.

The End

Made in the USA
Lexington, KY
21 September 2012